W9-BBW-273

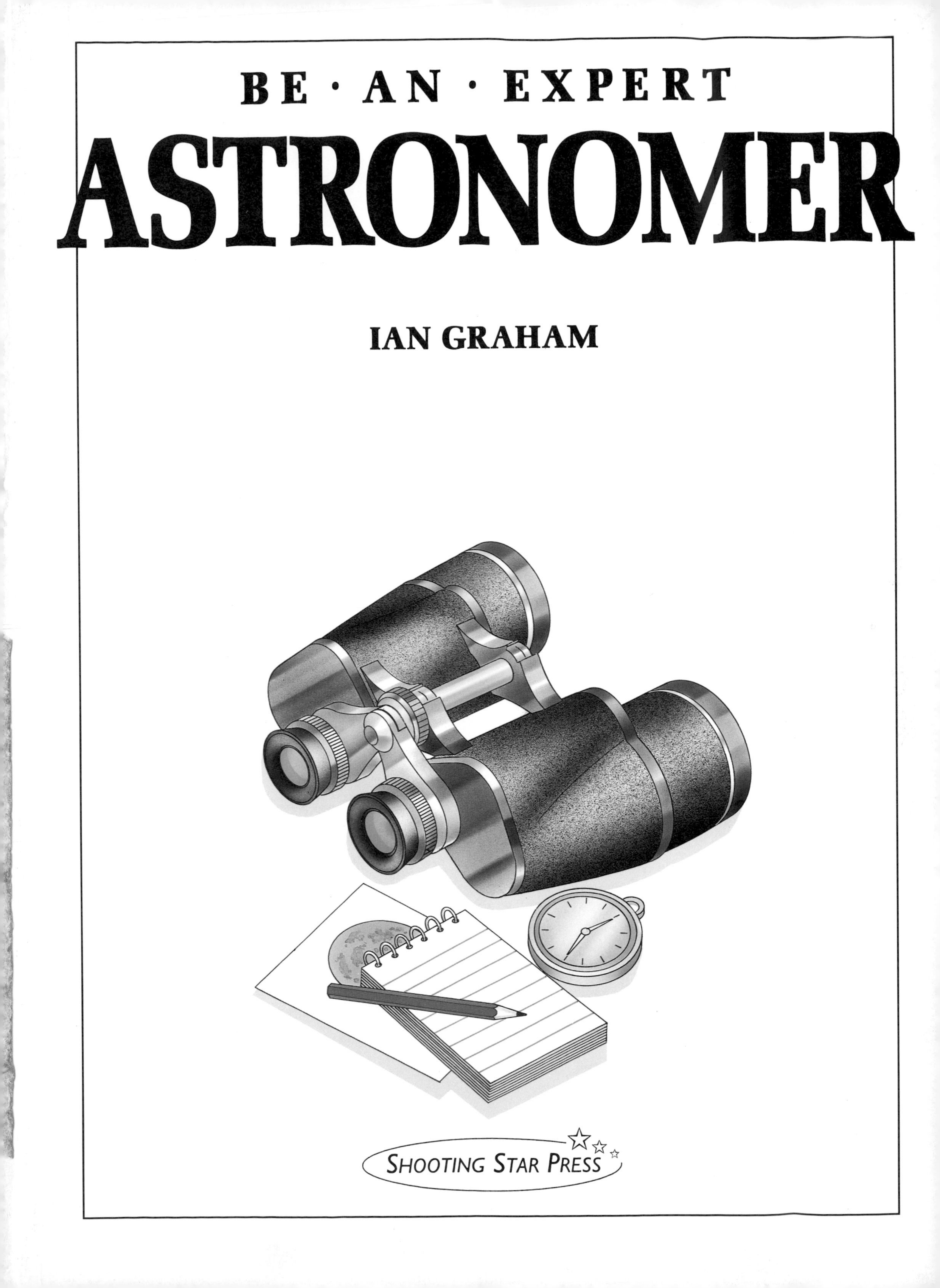

BE · AN · EXPERT

ASTRONOMER

IAN GRAHAM

SHOOTING STAR PRESS

This edition produced
in *1993* for
Shooting Star Press Inc
230 Fifth Avenue
New York, NY 10001

Design David West
Children's Book Design
Designer Stephen
Woosnam-Savage
Editorial Lionheart Books
Picture Researcher
Emma Krikler
Consultant Dr R.W. Forrest
Illustrator Ian Moores
Editor Roger Vlitos

The publishers wish to point out that all the photographs reproduced in this book have been either posed by models or obtained from photographic agencies.

Created and produced by
NW Books
28 Percy Street
London W1P 9FF

First published in the
United States in 1991 by
Gloucester Press

ISBN 1-56924-026-4

Printed in Belgium

Photocredits
Pages 6 top and bottom, 8, 12 top and bottom, 13 all, 16 top and bottom, 17 top and bottom, 18, 24, 27 and 29 top and bottom: Science Photo Library; pages 7 and 23: Roger Vlitos; page 10-11: Planet Earth Pictures; page 15 top and bottom: Spectrum Colour Library.

INTRODUCTION

Astronomy is the branch of science devoted to the stars, planets, and the vast distances that make up the Universe. People have been fascinated with the heavens since ancient times, but few had the chance to understand what they were seeing. This book gives you the basic information needed to become an astronomer. It also introduces you to some of the methods that the professionals use.

You do not need long and detailed special training before you can make exciting observations of extraordinary events. Nor is it necessary to have expensive equipment in order to be an active astronomer. However, it is important to learn about the Universe, stars, and how Earth fits into the system. Remember, some of the major discoveries in modern astronomy were made by amateurs scanning the night sky above their own homes. So go out under the stars on a clear night and study what you can see.

CONTENTS

USEFUL EQUIPMENT

FIELDS OF VIEW
The more a pair of binoculars or a telescope can magnify an image, the more powerful they are. At the same time the "field of view" is reduced. For example with the unaided eye one star in the constellation of Orion appears "fuzzy." With binoculars or a telescope this appears as the nebula (a gas cloud in space) it really is.

With just a little preparation and planning , you can get down to business. To start with, it is a good idea to put together some basic equipment like a watch, compass, and some star charts (see pages 20-21). Astronomical societies or magazines will let you know if something special, such as a comet, can be viewed and where to look for it. There is much that can be seen with the unaided eye, but a pair of binoculars or a telescope will reveal greater detail. These instruments can be mounted on a tripod to keep them steady. This will help you make drawings of what you see to go along with your astronomer's notes. These might come in very handy later on if you want to study your observations, compare them with friends, or show them to professionals. Remember, good notes are essential if you ever want to claim a discovery.

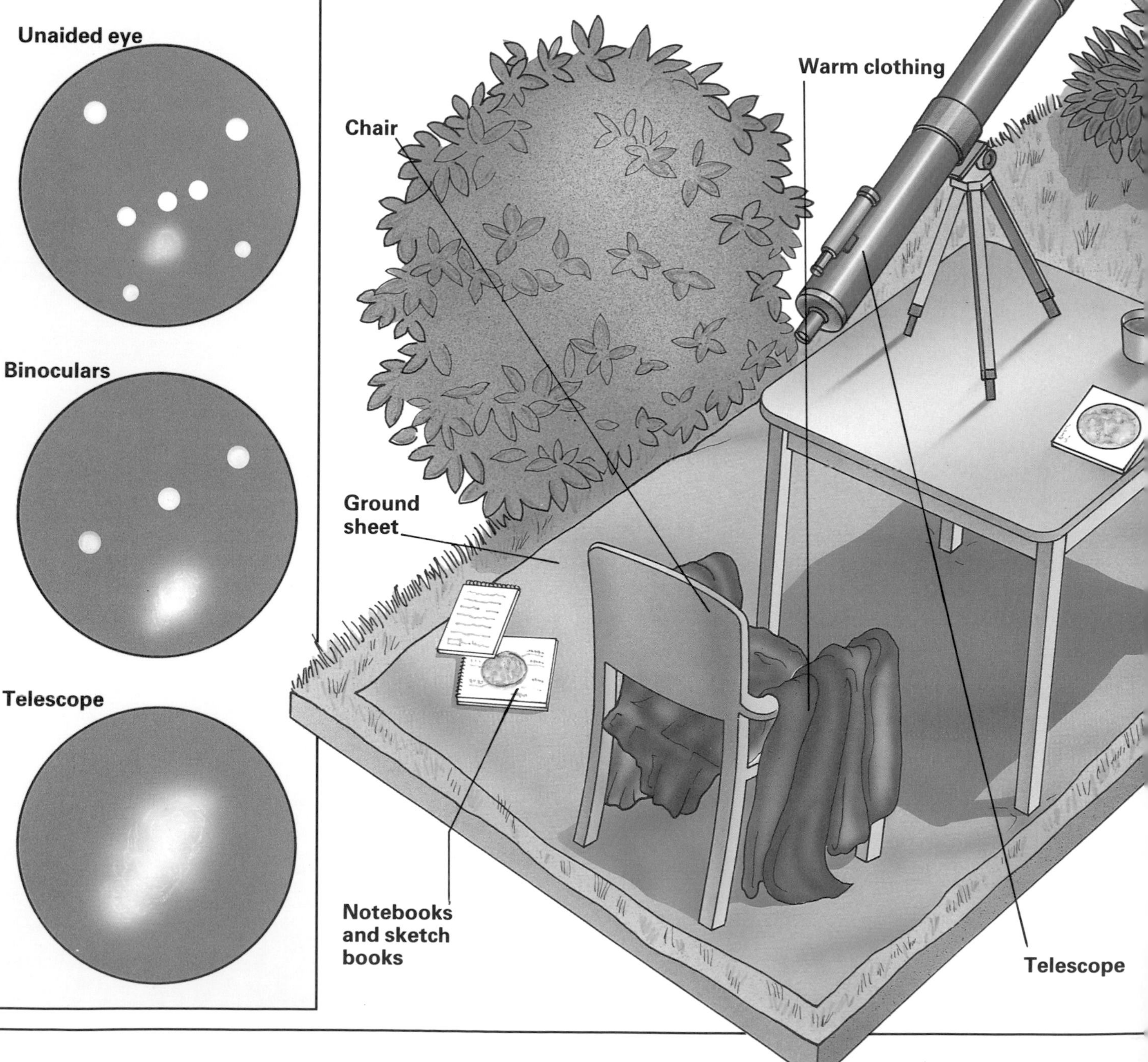

THE AMATEUR ASTRONOMER

Wear adequate clothes for an evening's observing outdoors, according to the season. Bring a thermos of hot drink and something to eat, too. Cover your flashlight lens with thin, red plastic. This will allow you to read star maps, use a planisphere, or draw in the dark. Otherwise, you may waste time waiting for your eyes to readjust to the starlight.

OPTICAL INSTRUMENTS

Don't be tempted to buy a small telescope. Binoculars are cheaper, lighter and easier to handle. A more powerful telescope may be useful later when you know your way around the night sky. You might also like to try photographing the sky or the view through a telescope. A medium-speed film (100-200 ISO) is best for planets. Fast films (400-1600 ISO) are suitable for stars and comets.

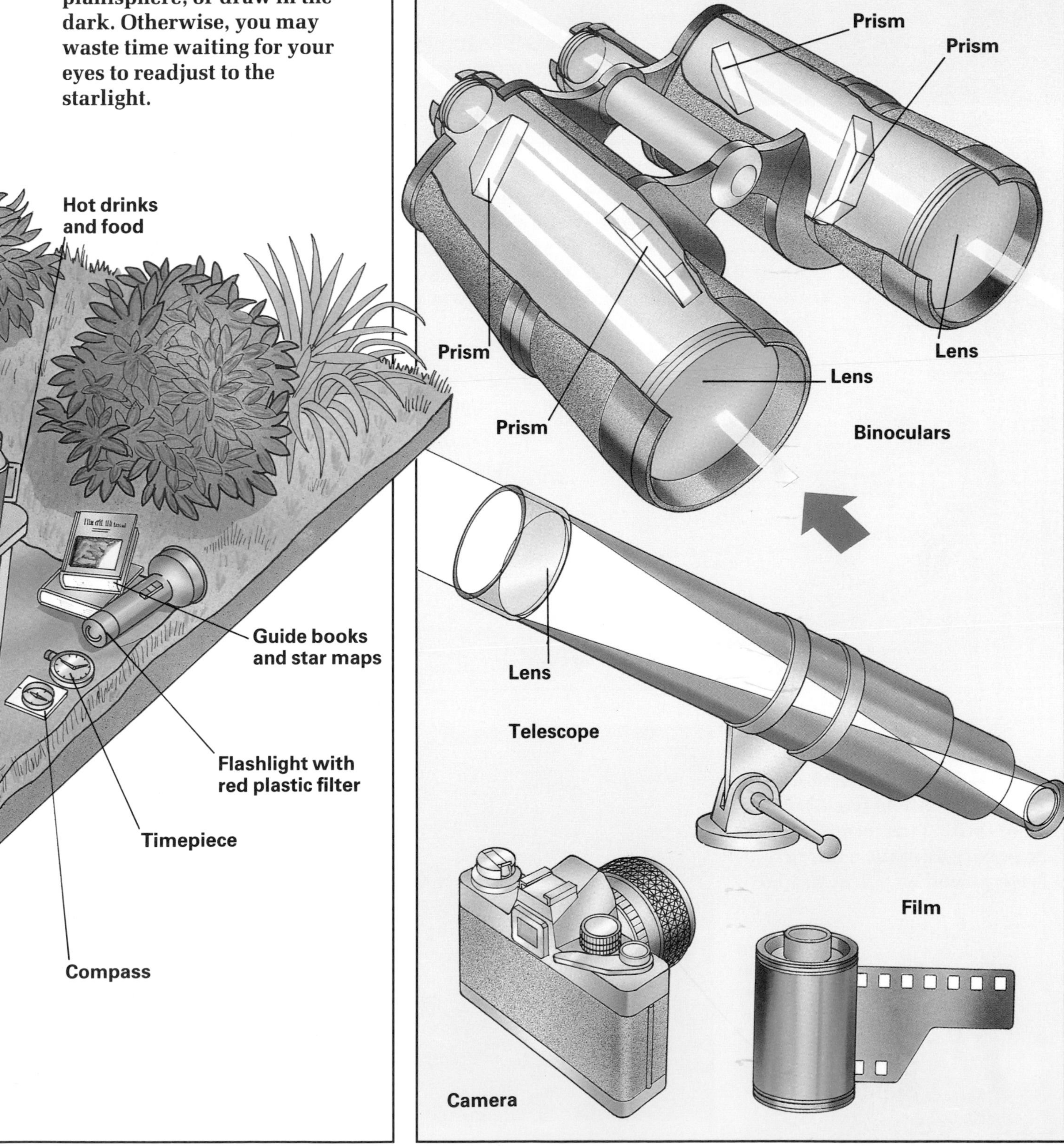

EARTH IN SPACE

Understanding how Earth moves in space is the vital first step in becoming an expert astronomer. Earth is the third planet from the sun and orbits at an average distance of 93 million miles. From here Earth is warmed just enough to allow water to flow as a liquid over most of the planet, forming the oceans. This is where life began and as far as we know Earth is the only planet where life exists. Satellites now enable us to see what Earth and its atmosphere look like from space. The blue sphere marbled with white clouds (see photo on left) looks attractive from space. But these clouds can hide the stars from view.

THE SEASONS

Regular changes in Earth's weather, the seasons, are caused by a tilt in Earth's axis. When the Northern Hemisphere leans toward the sun, it receives more heat for more hours in the day. While the Northern Hemisphere enjoys summer, the Southern Hemisphere, which tilts away from the sun, experiences winter. Six months later, when Earth is on the opposite side of the sun, the Southern Hemisphere is tilted toward the sun and it enjoys summer.

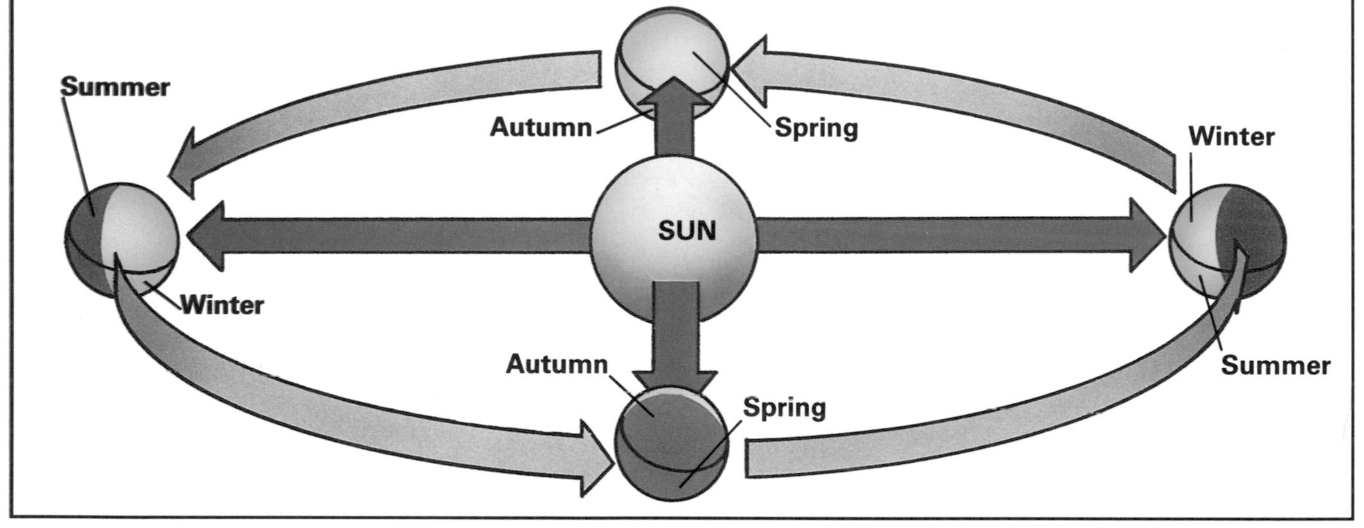

STAR TRAILS

Stars appear to drift across the night sky, but it is Earth that turns. This photo (right) was made with a ten minute exposure after the camera had been placed on a firm support.

EARTH'S ROTATION

Earth spins on its axis once every 24 hours. As a result of this rotation, the sun and all the other stars in the sky appear to rise in the East, follow a curved path across the sky and set in the West. Scientists have demonstrated this constant rotation by using heavy pendulums suspended from long wires which turn as they swing for days at a time. The direction of the swings changes as Earth rotates. The diagram below shows how to make a simpler version. This will create a pattern that is the result of rotation.

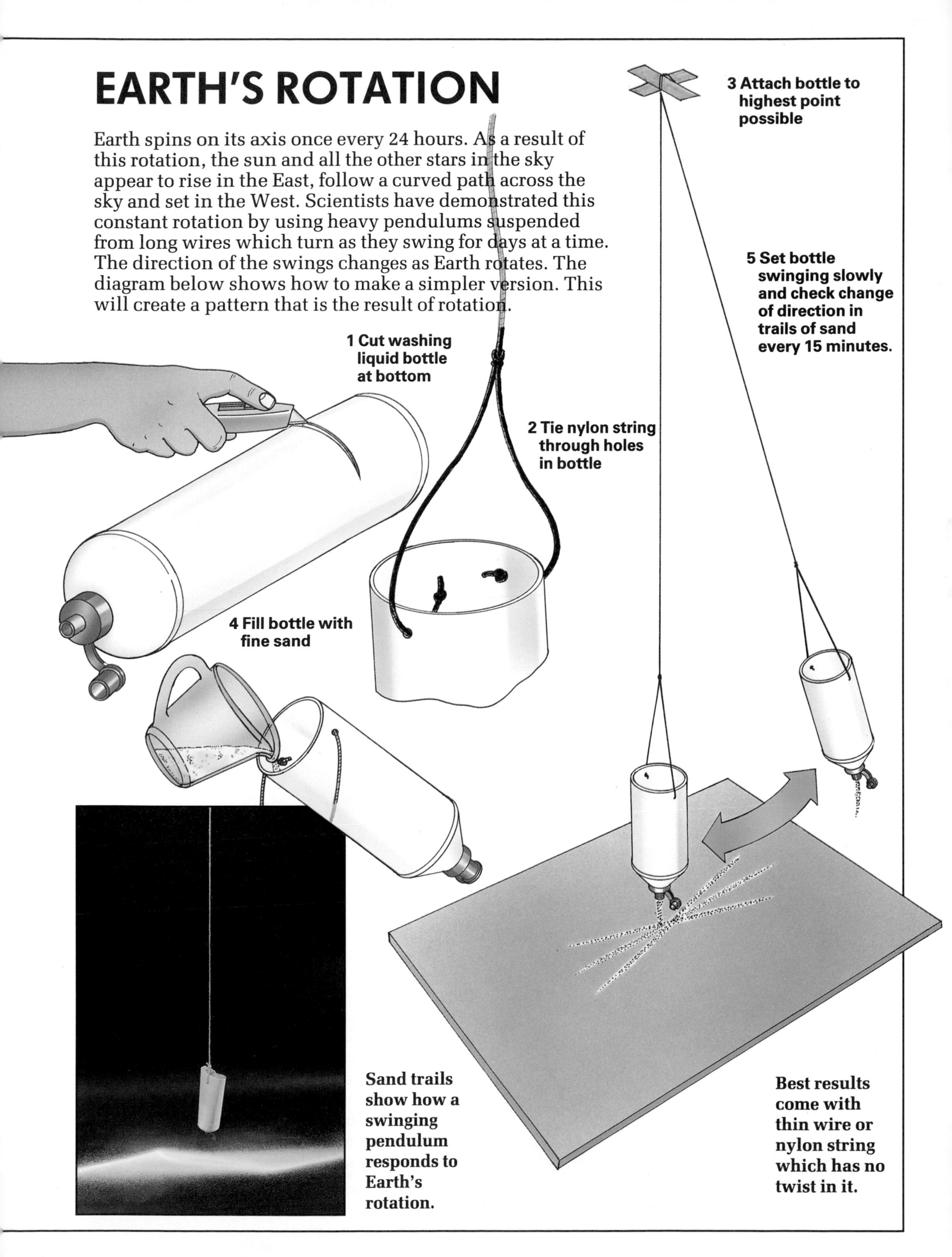

Sand trails show how a swinging pendulum responds to Earth's rotation.

THE SUN, OUR STAR

The sun is our closest star, a ball of gases about 865,000 miles across. It is 300,000 times bigger than Earth, and has a very powerful gravitational pull that holds the nine planets of our solar system together in space. This gravity is so strong that solids and liquids cannot exist inside the sun, especially at the core, where the temperature is 25 million °F. Above this is a radiative zone of hot gases under tremendous pressure where hydrogen is transformed to helium. This keeps our star shining because in every second the sun converts millions of tons of itself into energy. The upper surface of the sun is called the photosphere. Above this, long jets of hot gas in the chromosphere give it its flaming appearance.

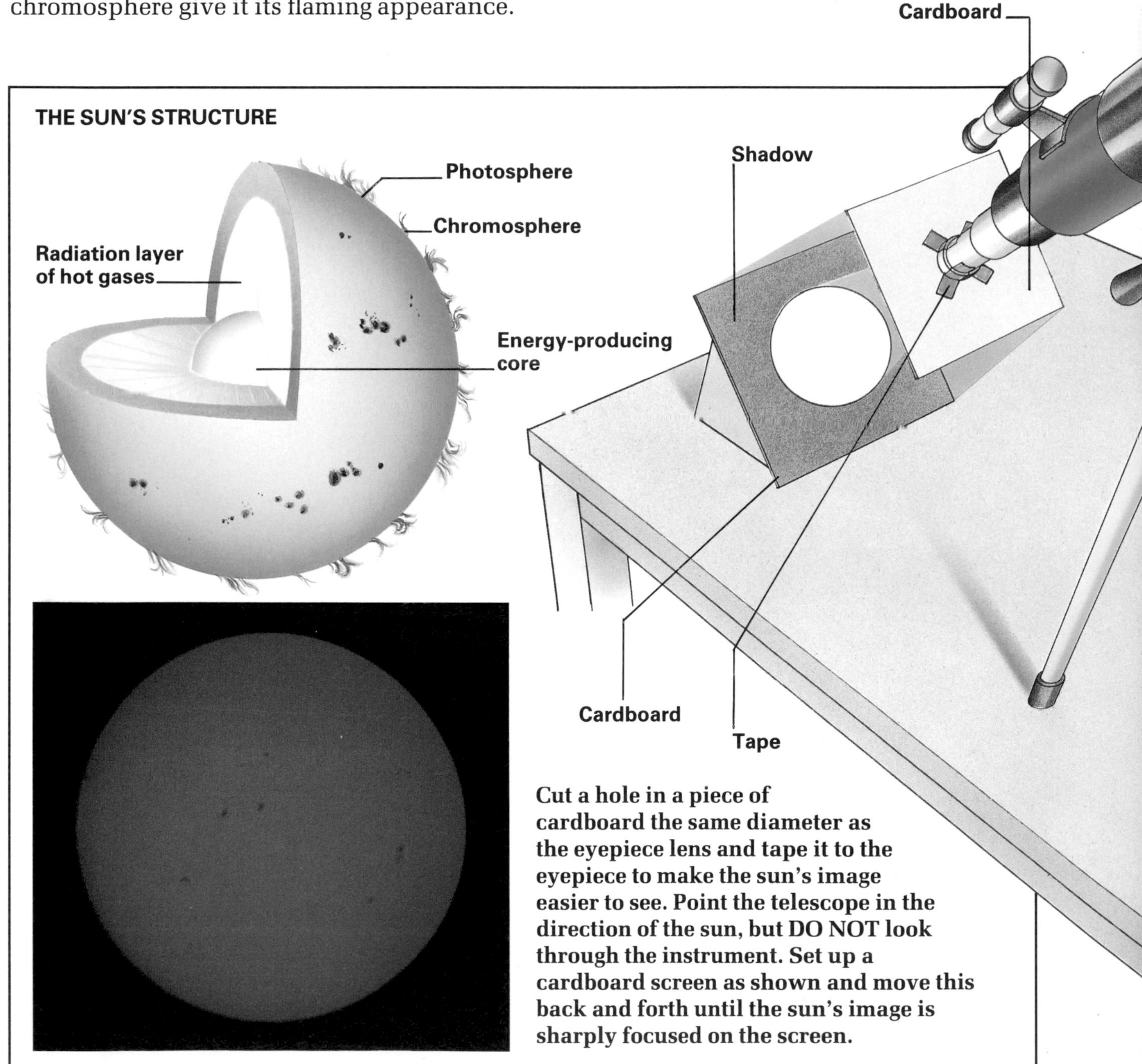

Cut a hole in a piece of cardboard the same diameter as the eyepiece lens and tape it to the eyepiece to make the sun's image easier to see. Point the telescope in the direction of the sun, but DO NOT look through the instrument. Set up a cardboard screen as shown and move this back and forth until the sun's image is sharply focused on the screen.

Telescope

OBSERVING THE SUN

The only *safe* way of making observations of the sun is to project its image onto white cardboard and view this. The illustration on the left shows the correct way to do this.

ECLIPSES OF THE SUN

As the moon passes between Earth and the sun, it casts a shadow called a solar eclipse. In a total eclipse, the moon blocks out the sun's surface, gradually revealing the variety of other features shown below.

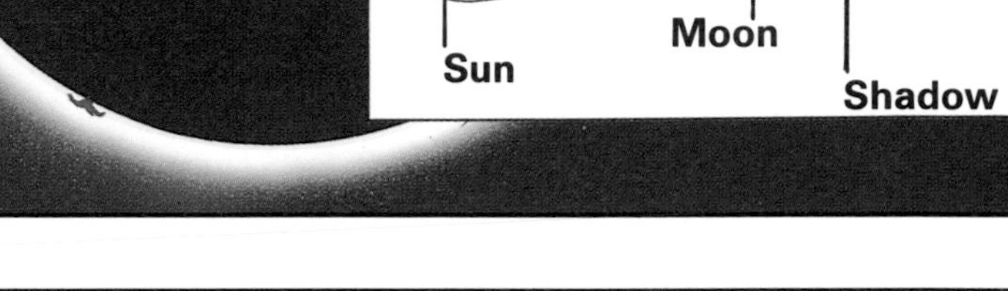

AURORAE

Charged particles streaming out from the sun form a solar wind (see yellow arrows in the diagram below) that distorts Earth's magnetic field. Particles trapped by the magnetic field (shown below as purple bands) spiral down to Earth's poles and collide with the upper atmosphere causing it to glow. The resulting colorful light display in the sky is called the *aurora borealis* or northern lights near the North Pole and the *aurora australis* or southern lights near the South Pole. These lights can appear as bright as the full moon.

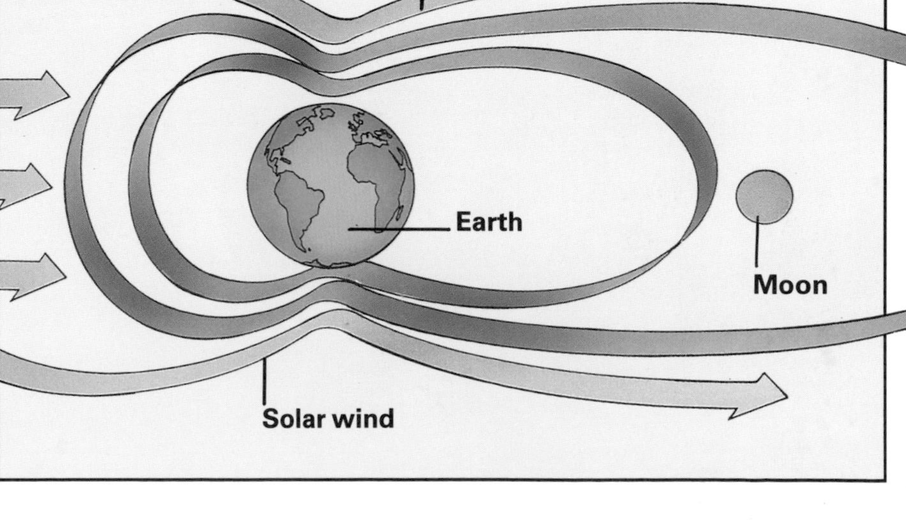

THE MOON

Earth's only natural satellite, the moon, orbits once every 27.3 days at an average distance of 239,000 miles. It takes the same time to spin on its axis and so the same side always faces Earth. The moon is one-quarter of the size of Earth, and so has a weak gravitational pull. As a result, its protective atmosphere has gradually leaked away and the moon is now a dead environment where the surface temperature in the daytime goes up to 220°F, and cools at night to −247°F. Astronomical telescopes turn the moon's image upside down and so maps of the moon are often printed upside down. Remember, if you are observing with the unaided eye, binoculars, or a "terrestrial" telescope, use a moon map printed with the north pole at the top.

THE MOON'S SURFACE
Binoculars show the moon's cratered surface well, especially near the dark side where the shadows are longest. The craters' rims make mountain chains as high as Mt. Everest.

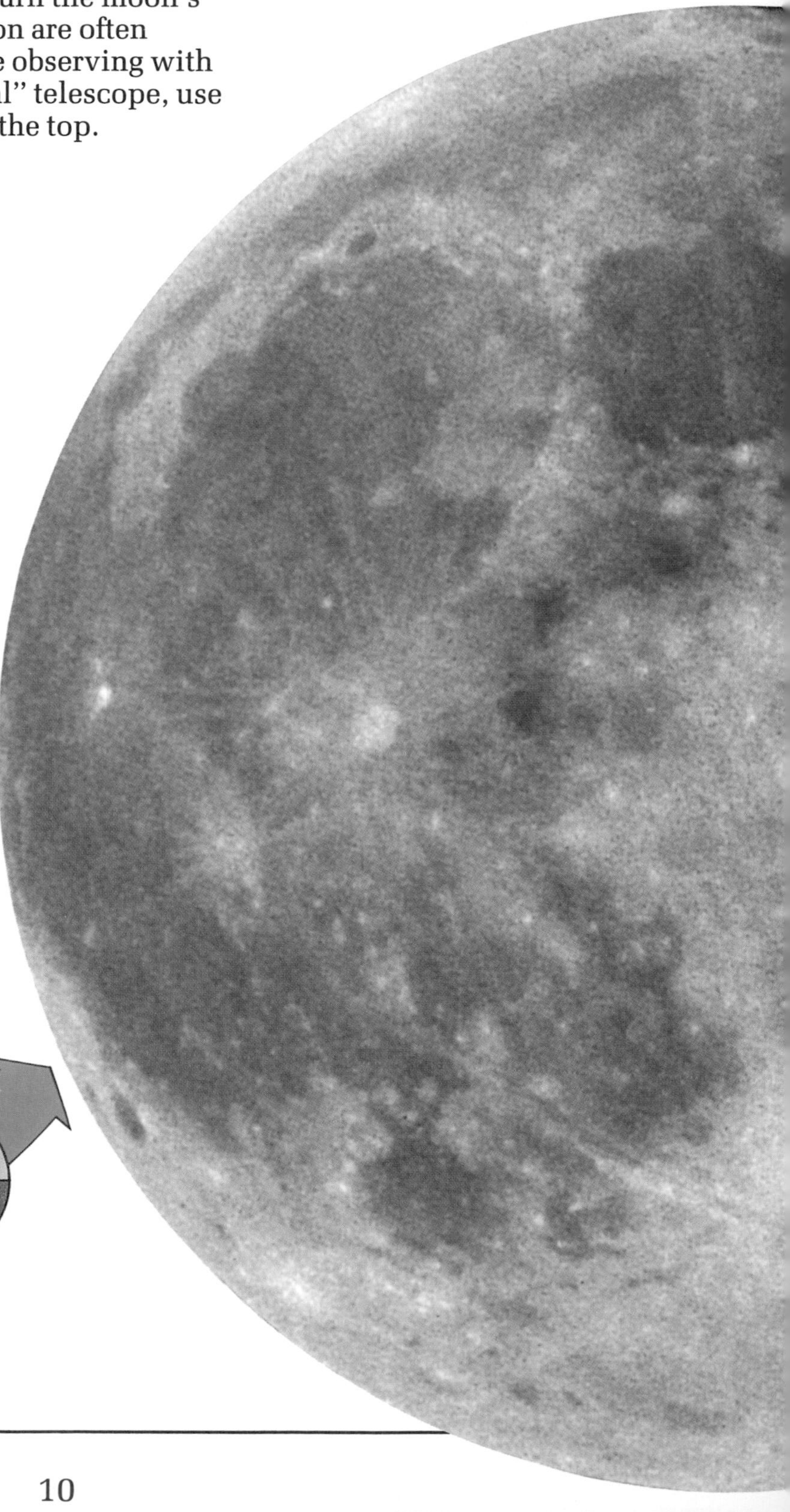

LUNAR ECLIPSE
As Earth and the moon orbit the sun, the shadow of each can fall across the other. If Earth's shadow falls on the moon, the result is a lunar eclipse. Sunlight cannot reach the moon directly, but light scattered by Earth's atmosphere turns it a spectacular copper-red color, and this can be seen from the night side of Earth.

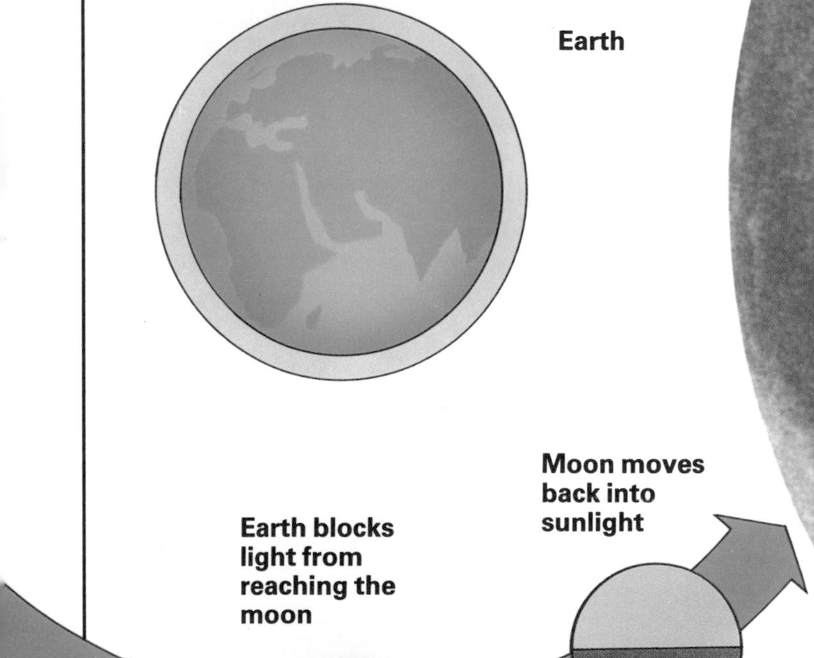

PHASES OF THE MOON
As the moon orbits Earth, it changes position with respect to the sun. We see different parts of the moon's sunlit face from Earth as it moves around us (see below). These apparent changes of shape are called the moon's phases. One cycle, from one new moon to the next, takes 29.5 days.

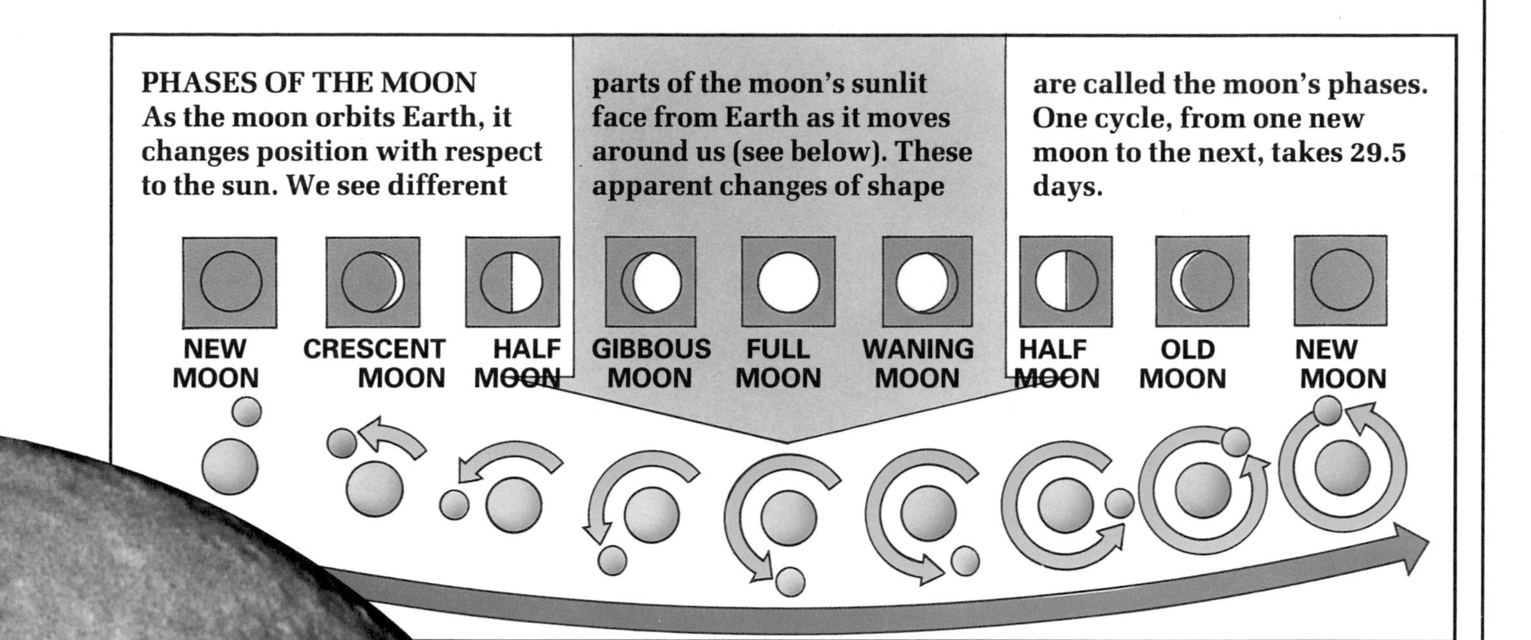

MAKING A REFLECTOR

You can experiment with a "reflector," or "mirror telescope," using the arrangement shown below. Use a magnifying shaving mirror to collect light from the full moon. Reflect it onto a mirror in a darkened room and enlarge the image with a powerful magnifying glass. This simple setup will not produce quality results. You would need special mirrors for that. However, it does show the basic way that "reflector" telescopes operate.

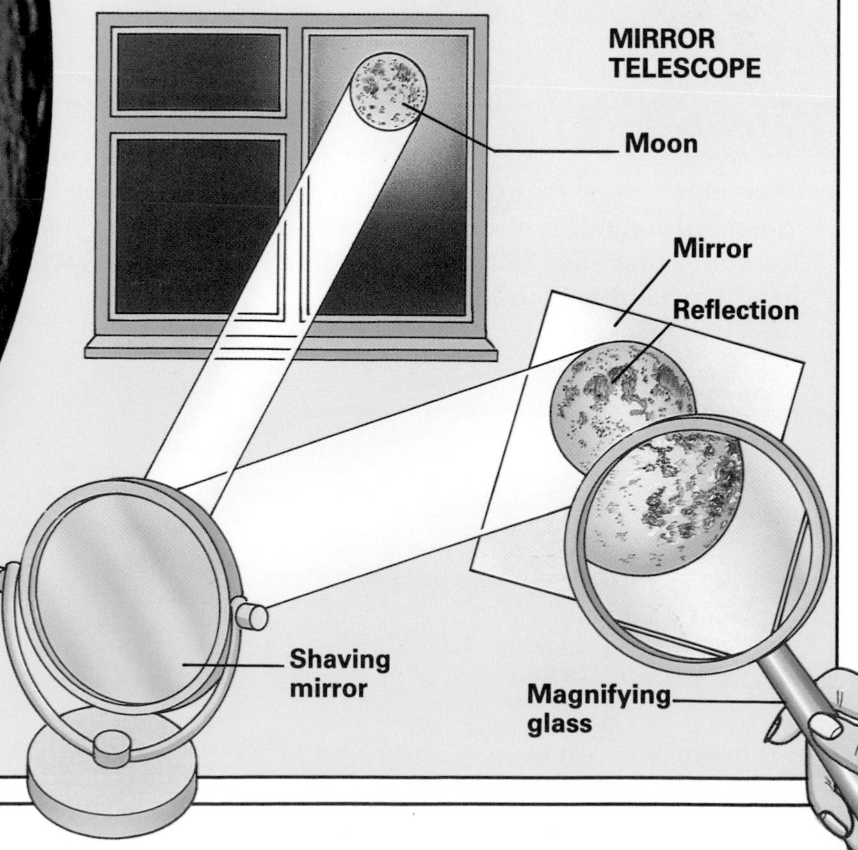

THE SOLAR SYSTEM

The solar system is our sun's family. It includes the sun and everything in orbit around it, from the nine planets and their 60 moons, to comets, asteroid belts, and meteors. The planets all orbit the sun in the same direction, counterclockwise when viewed from above the sun's north pole. Most have almost circular orbits on a plane called the "ecliptic" (see diagram below left) except for the slightly lopsided and tilted paths of Mercury and Pluto. We live relatively close to the heart of this vast disk of moving planets, but there is still much to observe and learn about the solar system.

MARS
Also known as the Red Planet, it has deep and long canyons on its rusty surface.

VENUS
Earth's near twin in size, this planet is the brightest planet in the sky.

THE SOLAR SYSTEM

The solar system is roughly 7,500 million miles wide, yet the sun, a mere 865,000 miles across, accounts for 99.9 percent of all the matter in it. It was born 4.6 billion years ago as a huge cloud of swirling gas.

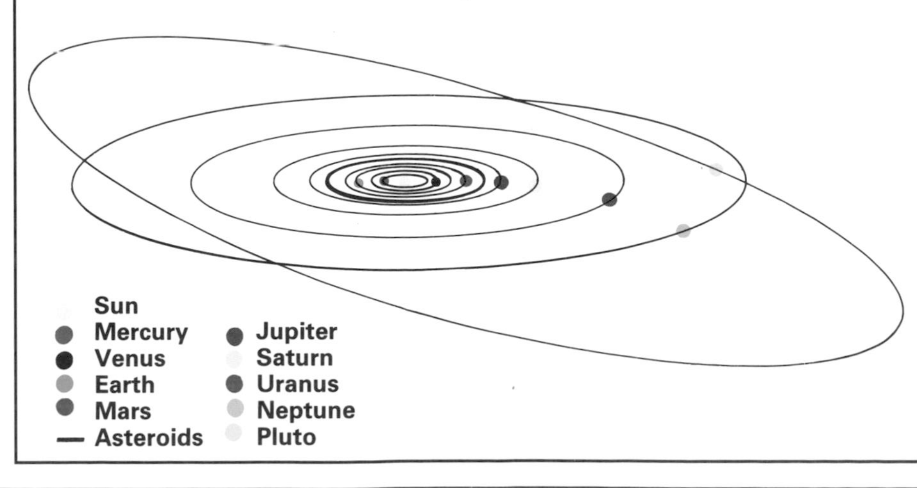

MERCURY
Because its orbit is so close to the sun, this cratered planet is difficult to observe.

JUPITER
Jupiter is the giant planet. The photo below shows one of its 16 moons which is the same size as Earth's.

SATURN
The beautiful rings of this planet are visible with binoculars.

NEPTUNE
Neptune has an atmosphere of gas disturbed by storms.

PLUTO
Tiny Pluto looks like a star through all but the largest telescopes.

URANUS
Nine vertical rings circle this gas giant.

SIZES OF THE PLANETS

The four inner planets are small and rocky. The five outer planets include the gas giants ranging from Jupiter, 11 times Earth's diameter, down to Pluto, one-quarter of the size of Earth. All are dwarfed by the sun.

FINDING THE PLANETS

The planets are not always visible to us in the night sky. This is because their positions change daily along their paths of orbit. Planets are not shown on star maps because they move so much. They appear to cross the sky near a line called the "ecliptic," which is shown on many star maps. Guidebooks showing the positions of the planets month by month are available from some bookstores.

VISIBILITY OF THE PLANETS

Here is a list of planets that shows the times and dates when they can be viewed in 1992. Astronomical data like this is normally presented in universal time (UT), which is also known as Greenwich mean time (GMT) and is the standard time of the Greenwich meridian (0° of longitute on maps). You will have to work out how this affects your own viewing times, or look for the local times in newspapers and astronomer's magazines.

PLANET	MORNING TWILIGHT	EVENING TWILIGHT
Venus	January 1st – May 7th	July 20th – December 31st
Mars	January 1st – December 31st	
Jupiter	January 1st – February 29th October 1st – December 31st	February 29th – September 4th
Saturn	February 16th – August 7th	January 1st – January 13th August 7th – December 31st

PATHS OF THE PLANETS

The planets orbit the sun at different speeds. The so-called "inferior" planets (those closer to the sun than Earth) orbit faster than "superior" planets (those farther away from the sun). As Earth overtakes or is overtaken by another planet, the planet appears to move in a very erratic way across the sky. It appears to slow down, stop, and move in the opposite direction for a time. It then reverses direction again and continues on along its path. The paths of an inferior planet, Venus, and a superior planet, Mars, are shown here with lines and numbers. You can check this for yourself by simply making a chart of the sky surrounding a planet's position, and then plotting the planet's position every three or four days.

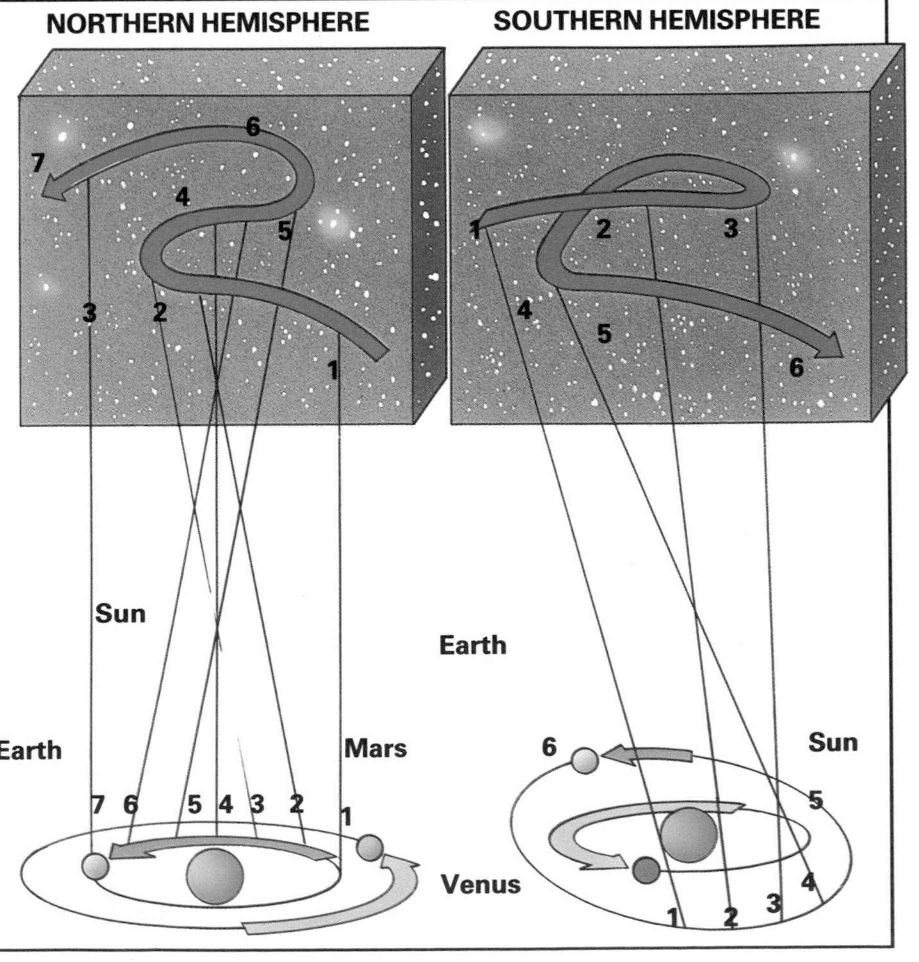

WHAT TO LOOK FOR

All the planets from Mercury out to Saturn can be seen with the unaided eye. Although they appear to be starlike points of light, their changing positions over a period of days, and their paths against the almost stationary background of stars, will reveal them to be planets. Through binoculars or a telescope, their disk shape confirms that they are planets. With binoculars, you should be able to see Jupiter's four largest and brightest moons orbiting close to the planet. Large telescopes show Jupiter's Great Red Spot, known to be a swirling storm, as well as surface features on Mars.

VENUS AND THE SUN
Because it is so close to the sun, the planet Venus is best viewed before dawn or after sunset, when it is both beautiful and bright in the morning or evening twilight.

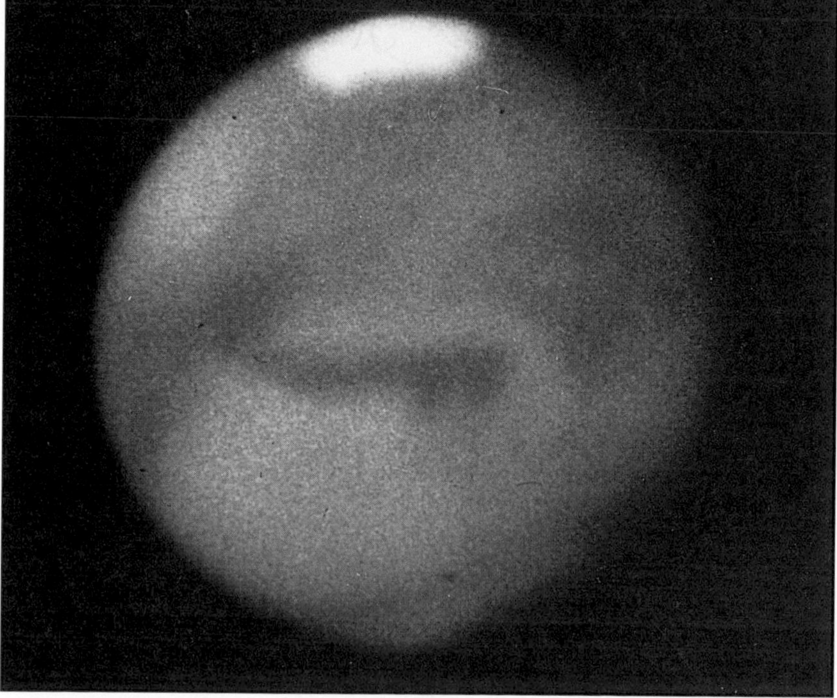

The photo above shows Saturn with its famous and beautiful ring system. These can be seen with binoculars, but not in the detail that we show here. With an even more powerful telescope you would be able to see that Saturn has several thousand rings that consist of ice and rock.

The photo on the left shows the large northern polar ice cap on Mars which is visible with powerful binoculars or a good telescope. Astronomers have noticed that this ice cap is shrinking.

COMETS

From time to time an object looking like a star with a tail appears in the sky. This is a comet. The solid portion of a comet is a mixture of water, ice, frozen gases, and rock. Comets travel far out in space away from the planets in elongated orbits. When their orbits bring them close to the sun, frozen gases on the rocky body vaporize and form the bright tail which always points away from the sun. Some comets are well known. Halley's comet, for example, returns every 76 years. Amateur astronomers have been very successful in discovering new comets, so keep your eyes and notebooks open.

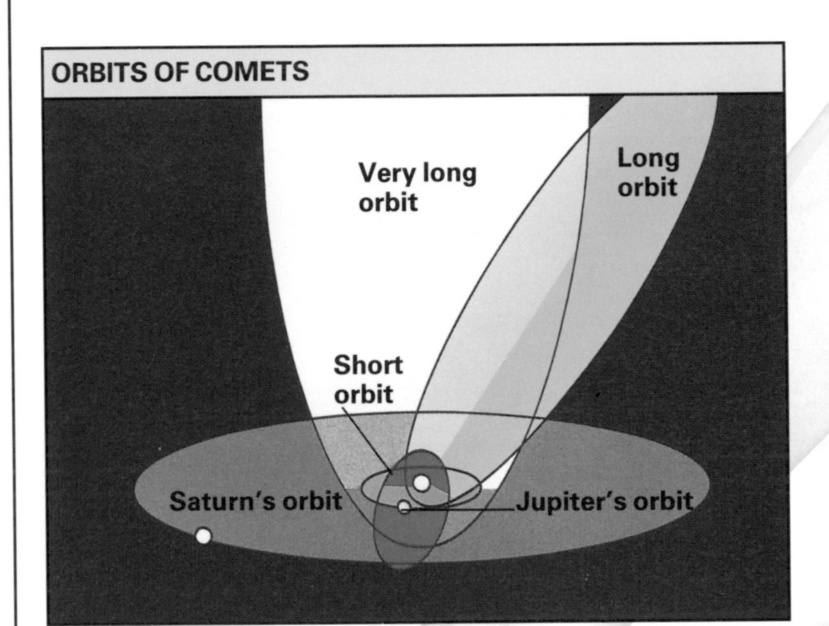

COMETS
A few comets are visible to the unaided eye. Others have to be viewed through binoculars or telescopes. Although many comets are well known, new comets are spotted from time to time and are always named after the person who first saw and recorded them.

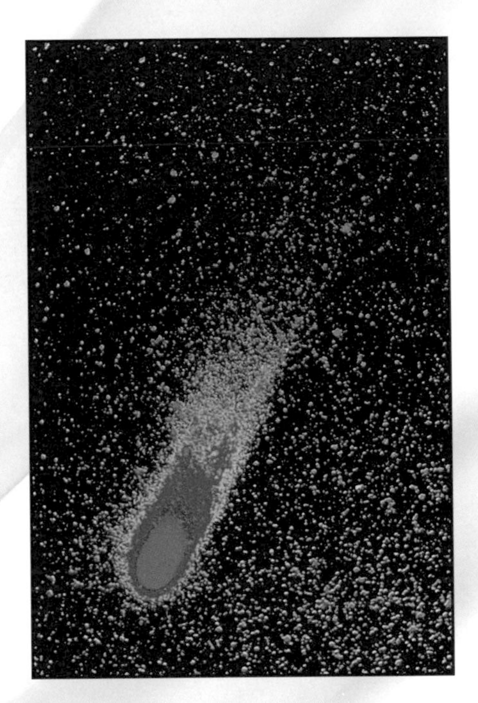

INSIDE A COMET
A comet's core is a mixture of water, ice, frozen gases, and rocks.

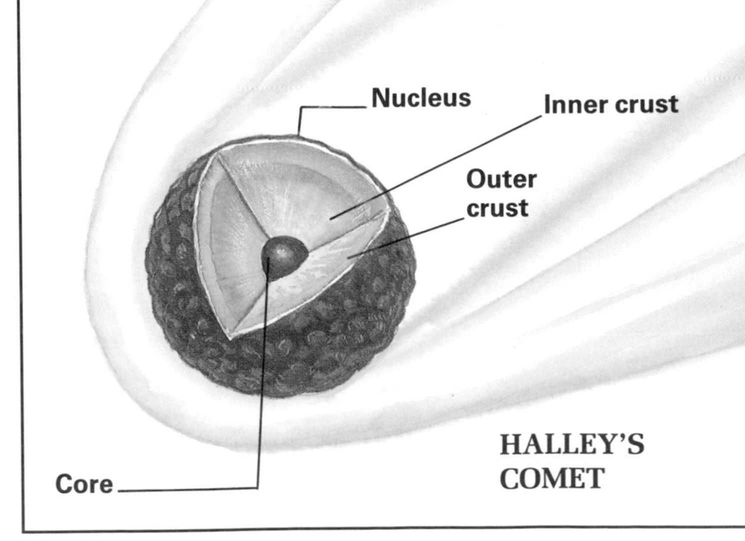

HALLEY'S COMET

ASTEROIDS

There are thousands of pieces of rock and iron orbiting in our solar system. We call them asteroids. One group of vast boulders orbits the sun in a "belt" between Mars and Jupiter. Another group, the Trojans, occupies the same orbit as Jupiter. This includes the largest asteroid, Ceres, which is over 600 miles across. A third group orbits close to Earth. The Martian moons, Phobos and Deimos, may be asteroids that have been captured by the planet's gravitational field.

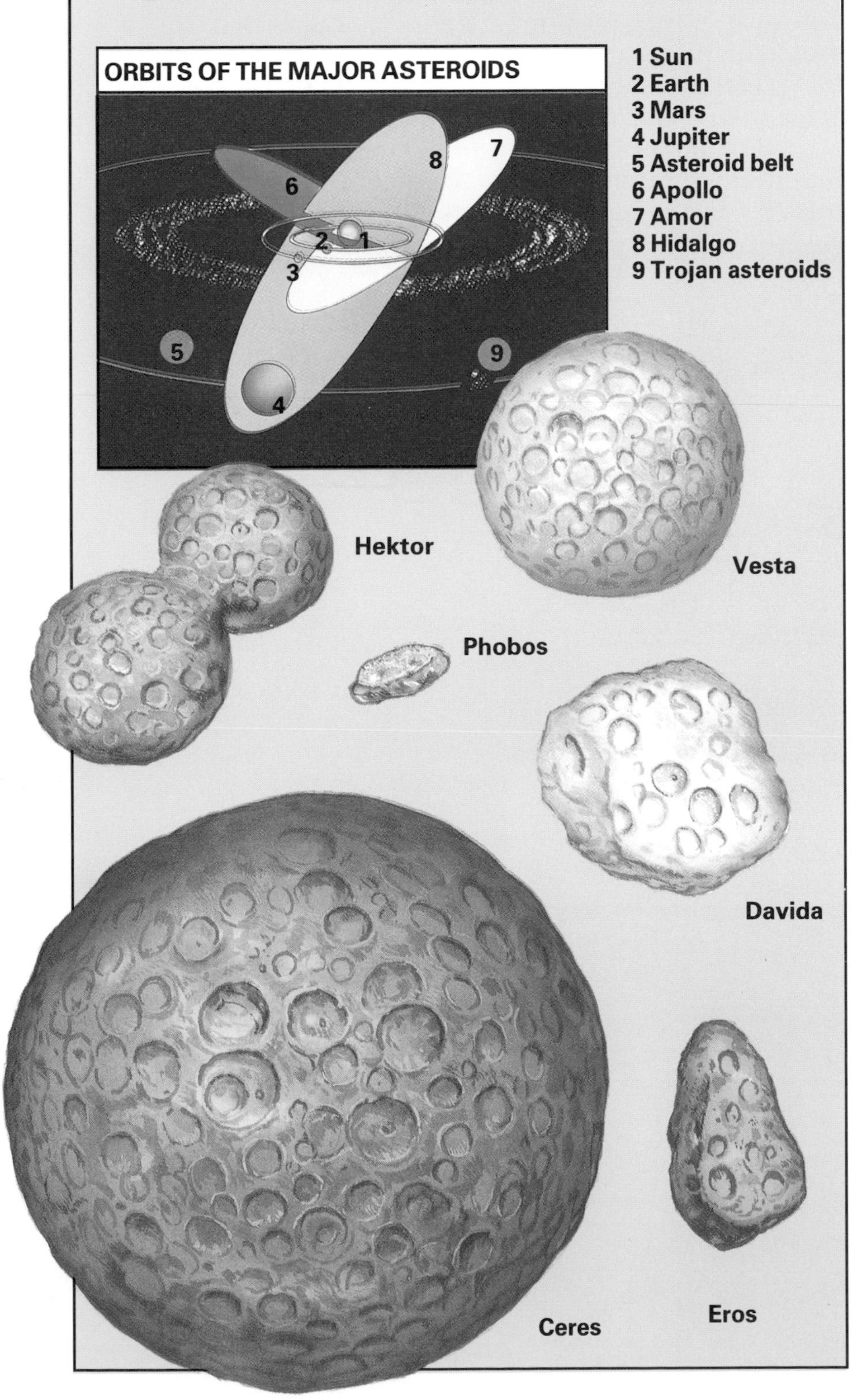

METEORS

Meteors, which are sometimes produced when asteroids collide, appear as streaks of light whenever chunks of debris from space enter Earth's atmosphere and burn up. Meteors can be seen on almost any night. Regular meteor showers also occur when Earth passes through a stream of particles left by a comet. The Orionid shower, for example, (October 16th-26th) is caused by particles from Halley's comet.

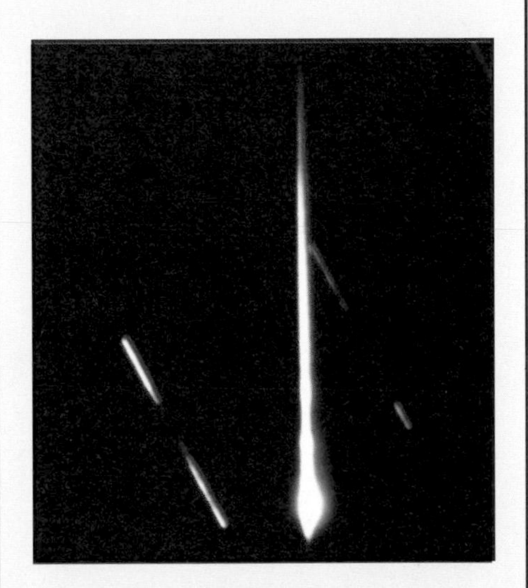

Because of their brief appearance, meteors are also known as "shooting stars."

ROCKS FROM SPACE
A meteor that reaches Earth without burning up is called a meteorite.

COLORS OF STARS

Every star has a subtle shade of color that can be seen with the unaided eye. Color is also a good guide to a star's temperature. The hottest stars are blue. Yellow stars are cooler, red stars are cooler still.

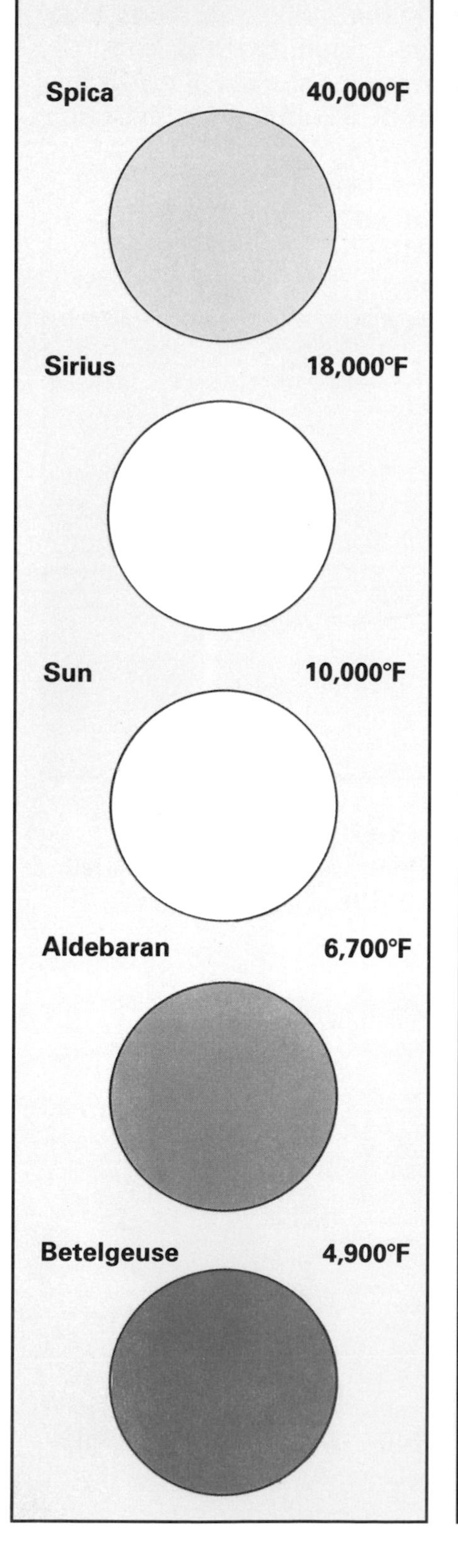

STARS

On a clear, moonless night, thousands of stars can be seen by the unaided eye from any point on Earth. As your eyes adapt to the darkness, subtle color differences become apparent. Some stars look red. Others look blue, yellow, or white. Through binoculars, these differences become more noticeable. Dimmer stars that are invisible to the unaided eye also come into view. You may notice that some stars vary in brightness over a period. Two of the main stars in the constellation of Cassiopeia are "variables." Mira in Cetus varies over 10 months from something that can be seen with the unaided eye when at its brightest to so dim that it can barely be seen even with binoculars. Other stars are actually pairs of stars called *binaries* that orbit each other. Other close pairs are simply called "doubles." Binoculars or a telescope are needed to separate most *binaries*, but some can be seen apart with the unaided eye.

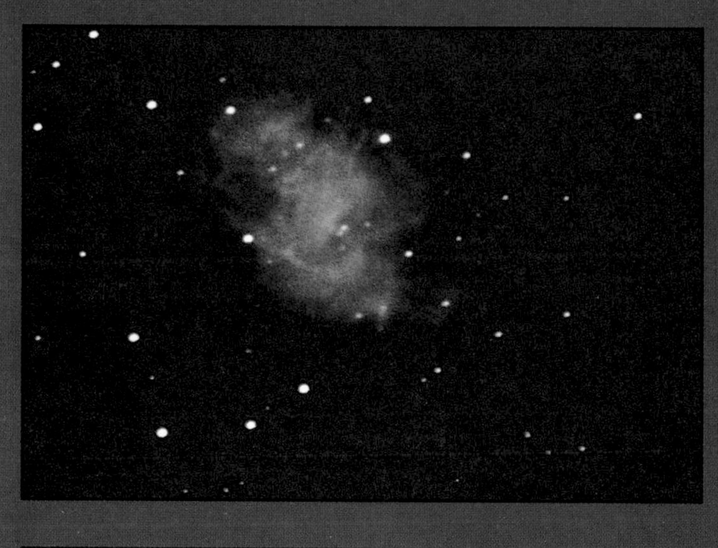

The Crab nebula in Taurus is the remains of a star that was seen to explode in 1054.

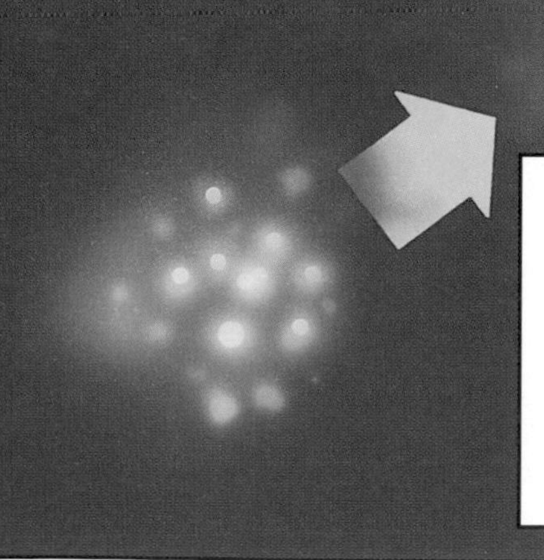

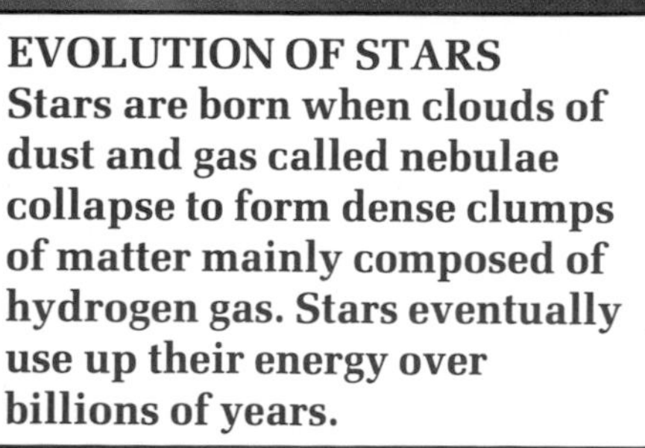

EVOLUTION OF STARS

Stars are born when clouds of dust and gas called nebulae collapse to form dense clumps of matter mainly composed of hydrogen gas. Stars eventually use up their energy over billions of years.

THE BEST WAY TO SEE

Stars are best observed on a clear night well away from city lights and smog. Try to wait half an hour to let your eyes adapt to the darkness.

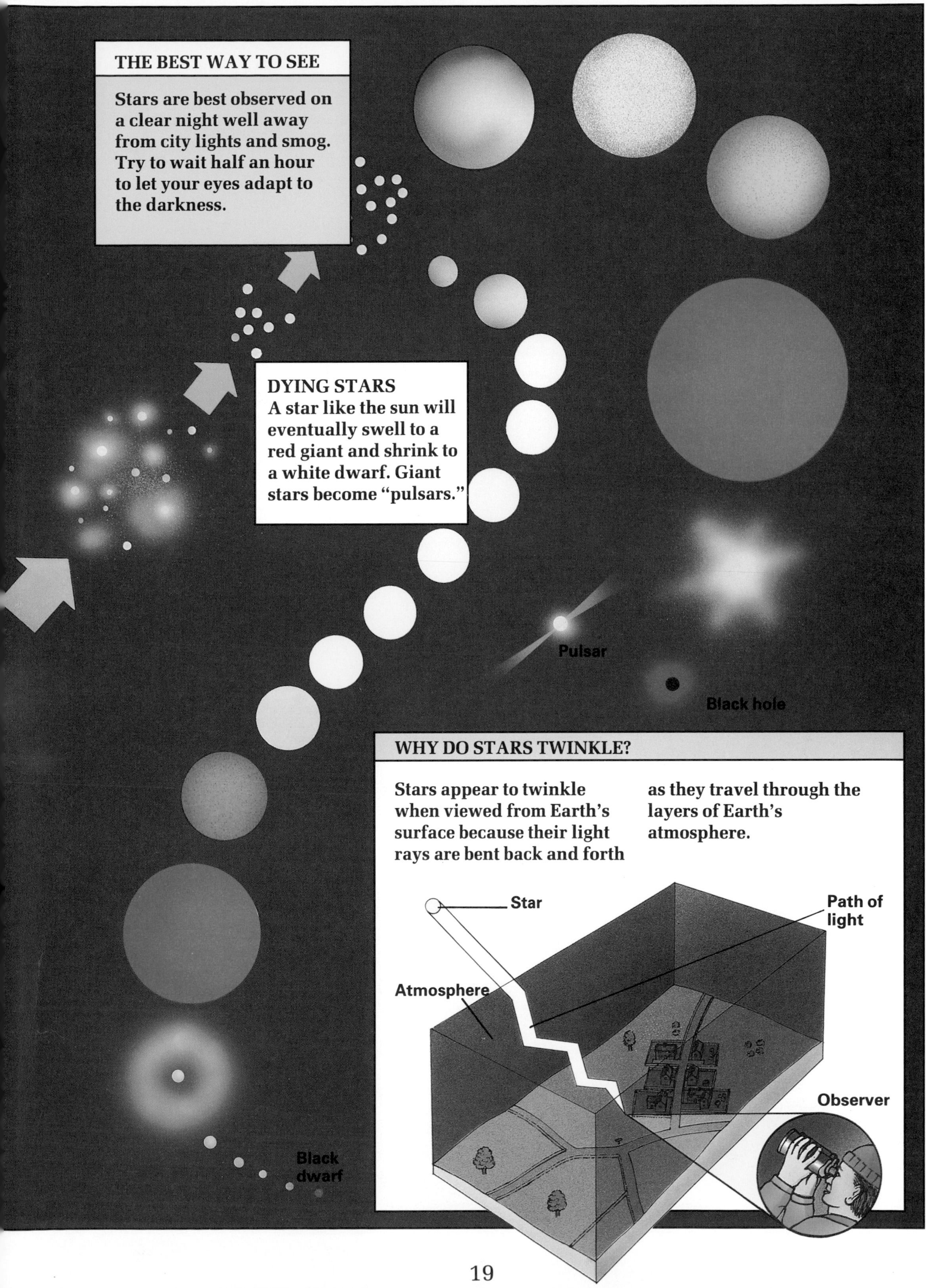

DYING STARS

A star like the sun will eventually swell to a red giant and shrink to a white dwarf. Giant stars become "pulsars."

WHY DO STARS TWINKLE?

Stars appear to twinkle when viewed from Earth's surface because their light rays are bent back and forth as they travel through the layers of Earth's atmosphere.

STAR CHARTS

The first astronomers saw patterns in the stars and named them after mythical animals, people, and gods. Star groups, or constellations, are still known by these names. The constellations and brightest stars are shown on these charts, one for each hemisphere. The stars are printed in bold type. As Earth revolves around the sun, different constellations appear, disappear, and reappear above us at different times of the year. To use star charts turn the appropriate chart until the current month is at the bottom. The constellations in the lower half of the chart should appear in the sky in the direction of Earth's equator.

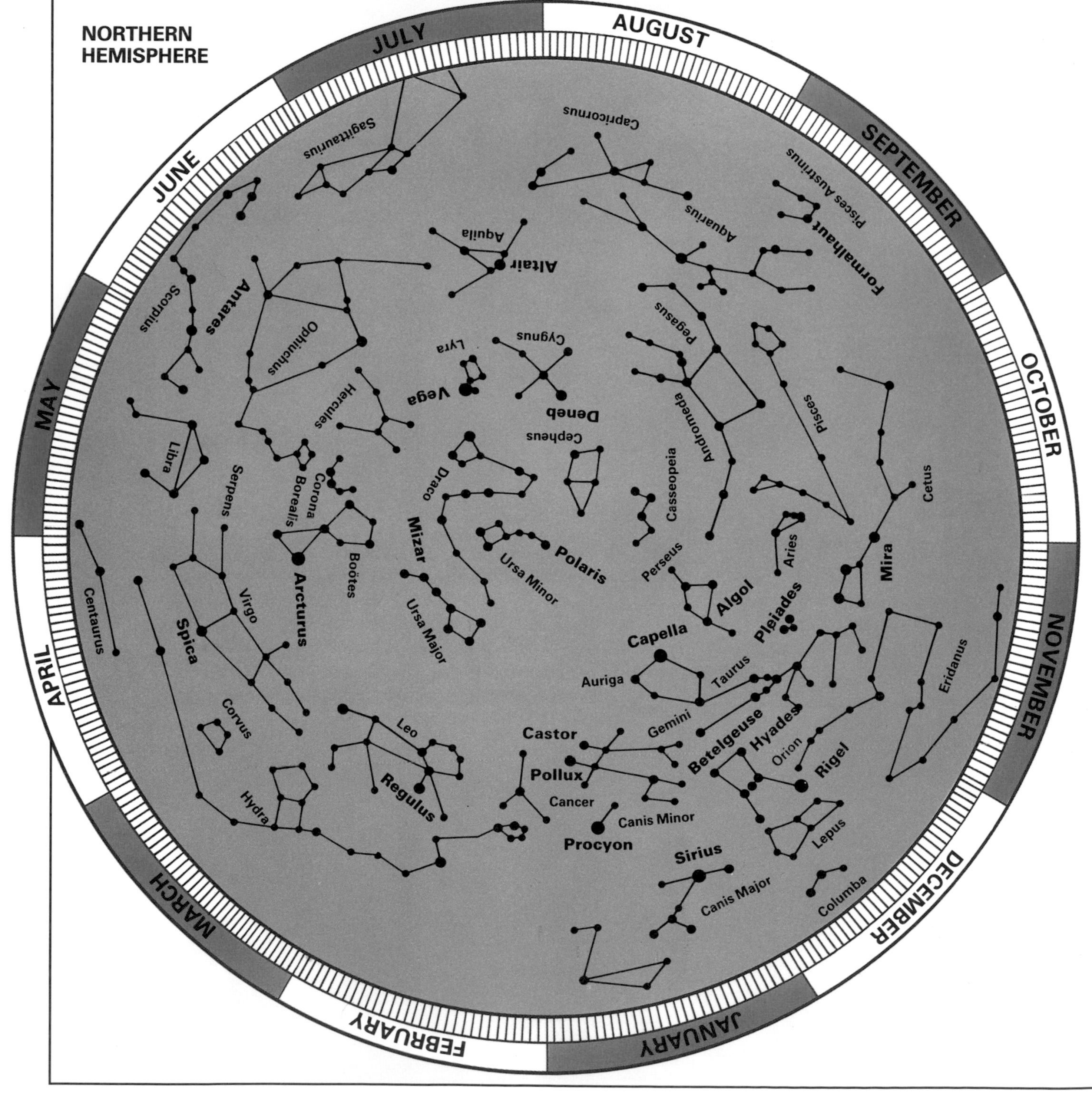

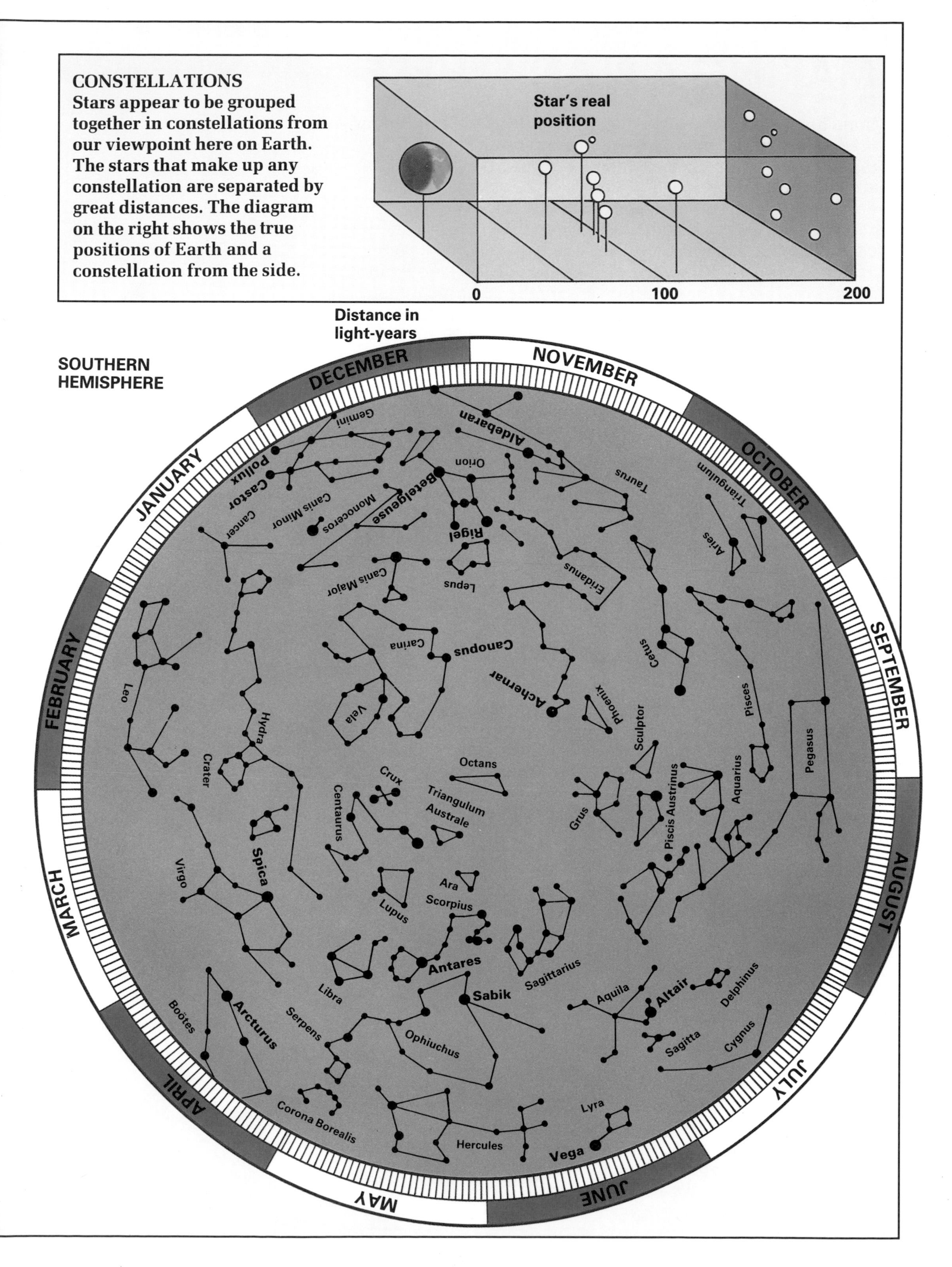
CONSTELLATIONS
Stars appear to be grouped together in constellations from our viewpoint here on Earth. The stars that make up any constellation are separated by great distances. The diagram on the right shows the true positions of Earth and a constellation from the side.
Star's real position
0
100
200
Distance in light-years
SOUTHERN HEMISPHERE
DECEMBER
NOVEMBER
OCTOBER
SEPTEMBER
AUGUST
JULY
JUNE
MAY
APRIL
MARCH
FEBRUARY
JANUARY
Gemini
Aldebaran
Orion
Taurus
Triangulum
Pollux
Castor
Cancer
Canis Minor
Monoceros
Betelgeuse
Rigel
Aries
Canis Major
Lepus
Eridanus
Cetus
Carina
Canopus
Achernar
Phoenix
Leo
Vela
Hydra
Crater
Sculptor
Pisces
Pegasus
Octans
Crux
Triangulum Australe
Centaurus
Grus
Piscis Austrinus
Aquarius
Virgo
Spica
Ara
Scorpius
Lupus
Antares
Sagittarius
Libra
Sabik
Aquila
Altair
Delphinus
Boötes
Arcturus
Serpens
Ophiuchus
Sagitta
Cygnus
Corona Borealis
Hercules
Lyra
Vega

MAKING A PLANISPHERE

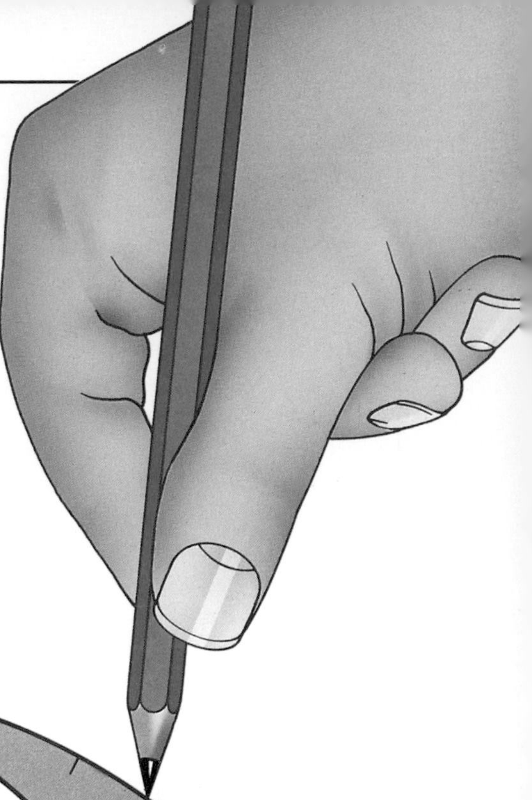

Star charts (see pages 20-21) show all the constellations and brightest stars (printed in bold type) that can be seen with the unaided eye in both hemispheres. Since not all of these are visible the whole year around astronomers use a handy device called a planisphere that shows where the stars and constellations can be seen at any given time of the year. Using the instructions on these pages you can make your own planisphere. First, draw the shape you see below onto a piece of thin cardboard and mark off the 24 hours of the day around the edge of the disk. Start with midnight at the top and proceed counterclockwise so that noon is marked at the bottom. Now proceed to the other stages.

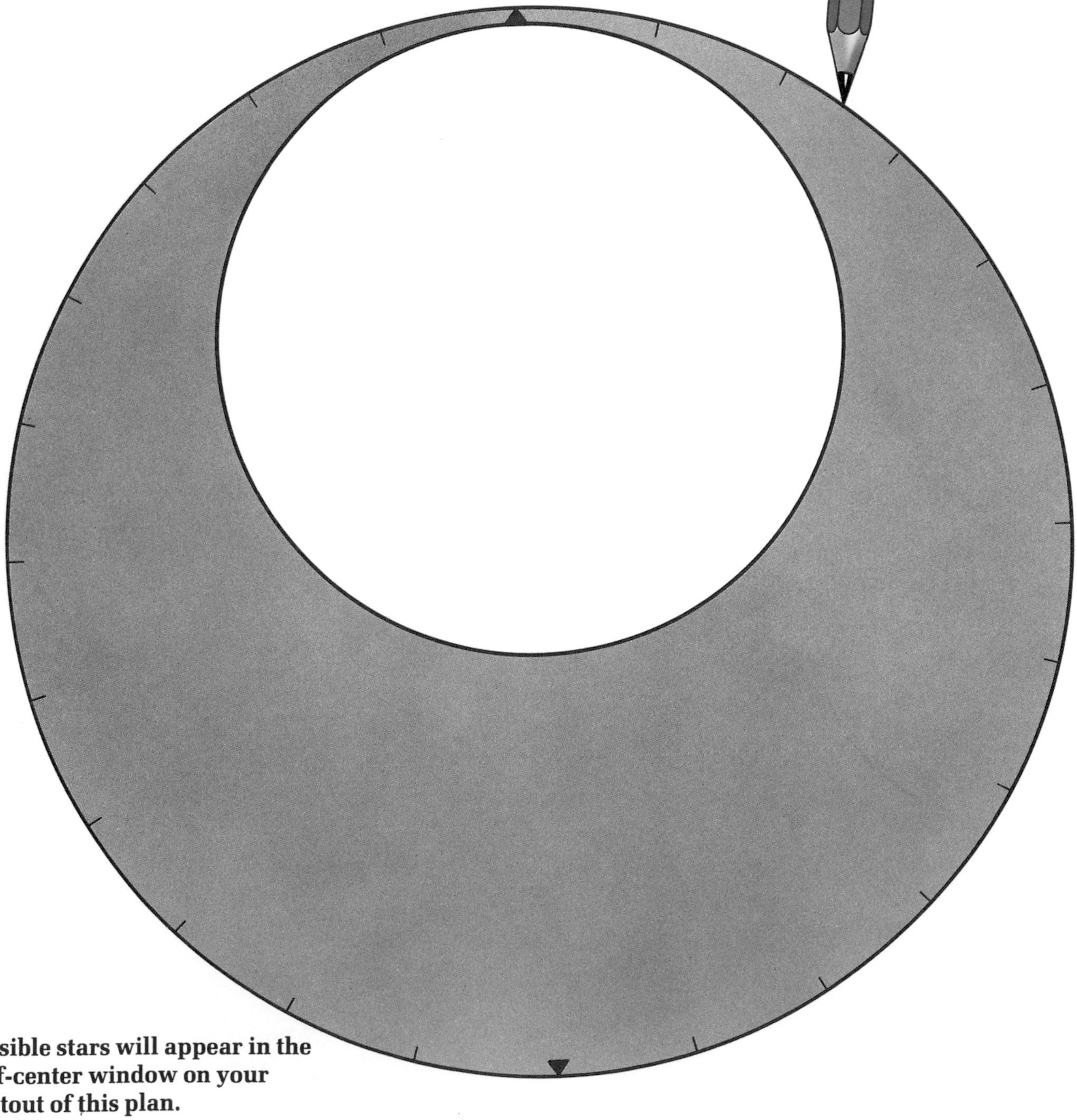

Visible stars will appear in the off-center window on your cutout of this plan.

WHAT TO DO

Trace the fixed positions of the stars in their constellations from the appropriate star chart on page 20 or 21, complete with the months of the year around the edge (1). Transfer the plan opposite onto cardboard, cut out the off-center window and cover with clear plastic (2). Stick the star chart tracing onto white cardboard. Pierce the center of both pieces of cardboard and fix them together with a butterfly pin.

MAKING A PLANISPHERE

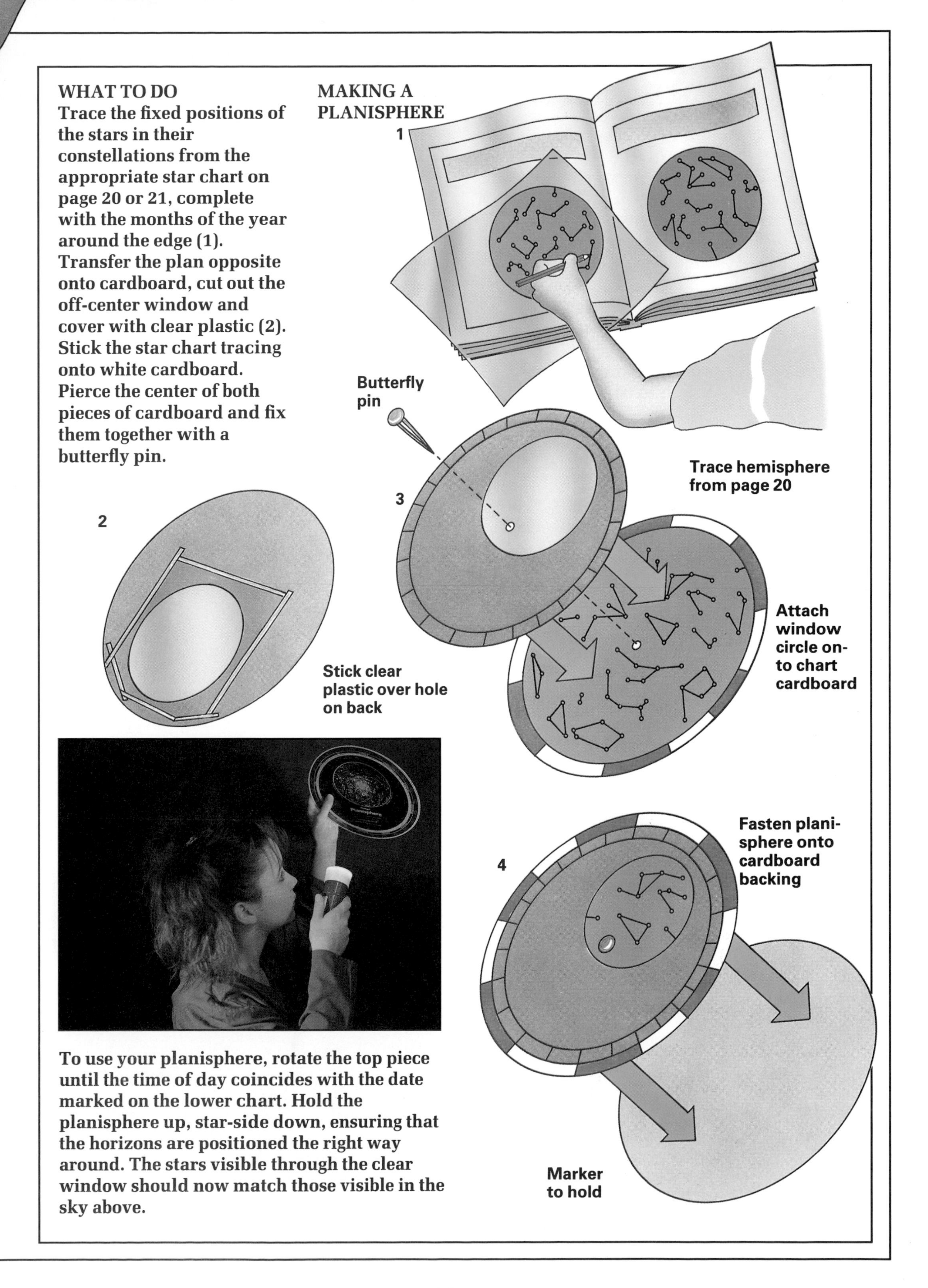

To use your planisphere, rotate the top piece until the time of day coincides with the date marked on the lower chart. Hold the planisphere up, star-side down, ensuring that the horizons are positioned the right way around. The stars visible through the clear window should now match those visible in the sky above.

DEEP IN SPACE

Many objects far out in space can be seen with the unaided eye, but binoculars or a telescope are helpful. With them you will notice the changing size of a variable star or the true number of stars in a cluster. Other objects are invisible to us, but we can detect them with special equipment. For example, "black holes" are the remains of massive stars that have collapsed. They suck other stars inside where their light cannot escape. Only X rays emerge to signal a black hole's position. These pages show some of the amazing objects which exist in space.

The Pleiades, or "Seven Sisters," (see below) is an open cluster of stars visible to the naked eye.

GLOBULAR CLUSTERS
Vast clumps of up to a million stars which mostly lie outside the disk of the Milky Way.

NOVAE
A burst of starlight, called a nova, is the result of gas from a red giant exploding off its white dwarf companion.

PULSATING STARS
Many variable stars change brightness over several months, but Cepheid variables require only days or weeks to do so. As they grow and shrink with enormous variations in their size, they also change color. The link between the rate of pulsing and the star's brightness can be used to measure the star's distance from Earth.

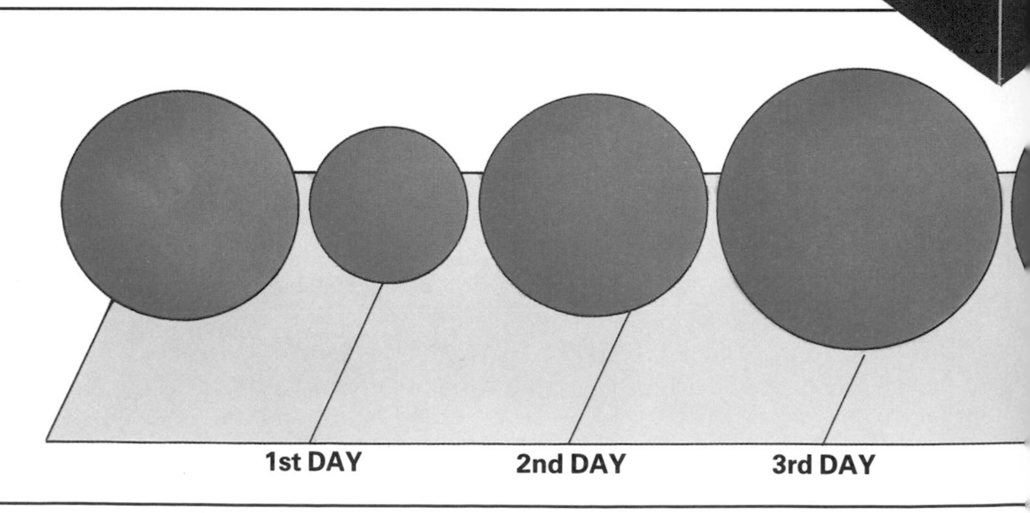

OPEN CLUSTERS
Groups of striking stars visible to the unaided eye in both hemispheres.

PLANETARY NEBULAE
This is a gas thrown off by what was once a red giant star.

PULSARS
The dense, spinning cores of collapsed stars which send out searchlightlike beams of radio waves.

QUASARS
Quasars are the very energetic cores of certain distant galaxies, and among the most distant objects we can see.

BLACK HOLES
Collapsed stars that can suck in other stars and trap their light.

HOW TO OBSERVE THEM

Variable stars are best observed by comparing them to unchanging stars nearby over a period of weeks. Some open clusters can be seen with the unaided eye, but binoculars will reveal more stars. The most distant globular clusters look like faint red stars, and require the power of a professional telescope to show any detail.

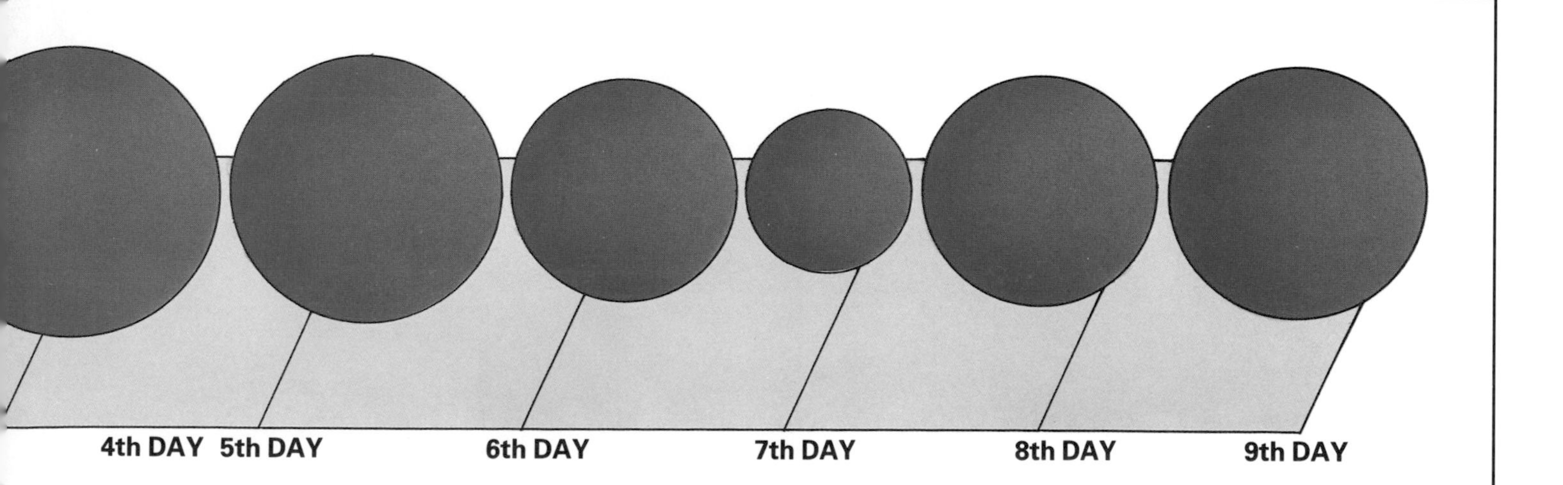

THE MILKY WAY

It is important for an astronomer to know what lies both in and outside our galaxy. Although the stars in the sky seem to be so far away that they are separate from us, the sun and almost all of the stars that we can see actually belong to a single star system called the Milky Way galaxy. The Milky Way contains about 300 trillion stars mingled with clouds of gas and dust. Its shape is similar to a pair of plates placed rim to rim, forming a flattened disk. If we could see it from above, it would look like a vast spiral of light slowly spinning through space. It is so big that even if we could travel at the speed of light, it would take 100,000 years to cross from one side to the other.

WHAT YOU CAN SEE

In some directions, the sky is dense with stars. This is because we are looking through the disk of stars that make up the Milky Way. In other directions, there are few stars against the black backdrop of space. This is the view out of the galaxy, either above it or below the disk of the Milky Way, where there are fewer visible stars.

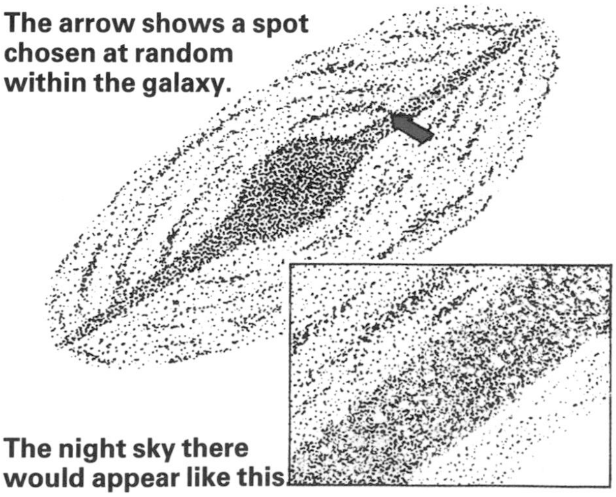

The arrow shows a spot chosen at random within the galaxy.

The night sky there would appear like this

HOW TO SEE IT

The Milky Way forms a hazy band of light across the sky. In the northern sky, it passes through Auriga, Cassiopeia, and Cygnus. In the southern sky, it passes through Vela, Crux, and Sagittarius. It shows up at its best on a cloudless, moonless night, away from city lights.

THE GALAXY'S CENTER

The center of the galaxy is 30,000 light years away in the direction of the constellation Sagittarius. It appears as a dense group of stars in the photo below.

WHERE WE ARE

The solar system (see box below) is situated in one of the spiral arms of the galaxy about two-thirds of the way out from the center. As you can see in this side view, most of the stars lie within the disk shape.

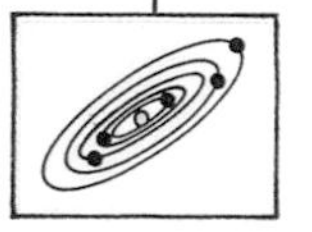

Our solar system

CENTER OF GALAXY

GALAXIES

Most of the stars we can see belong to the Milky Way, but some of the pinpoints of light in the sky are not just stars. They are other galaxies that lie far beyond our own star system. The Milky Way belongs to a cluster of about 30 of these galaxies called "the local group." Astronomers have found many thousands of other clusters in deepest space. Some of them contain thousands of galaxies. The largest and closest galaxies in our cluster such as the Andromeda galaxy, also known as M31, can be seen with the unaided eye, but many of the more distant galaxies can only be observed by powerful professional telescopes.

TYPES OF GALAXIES
In the 1920s, the U.S. astronomer Edwin Hubble classified all galaxies as one of three types – elliptical (E), spiral (S), and irregular (I).

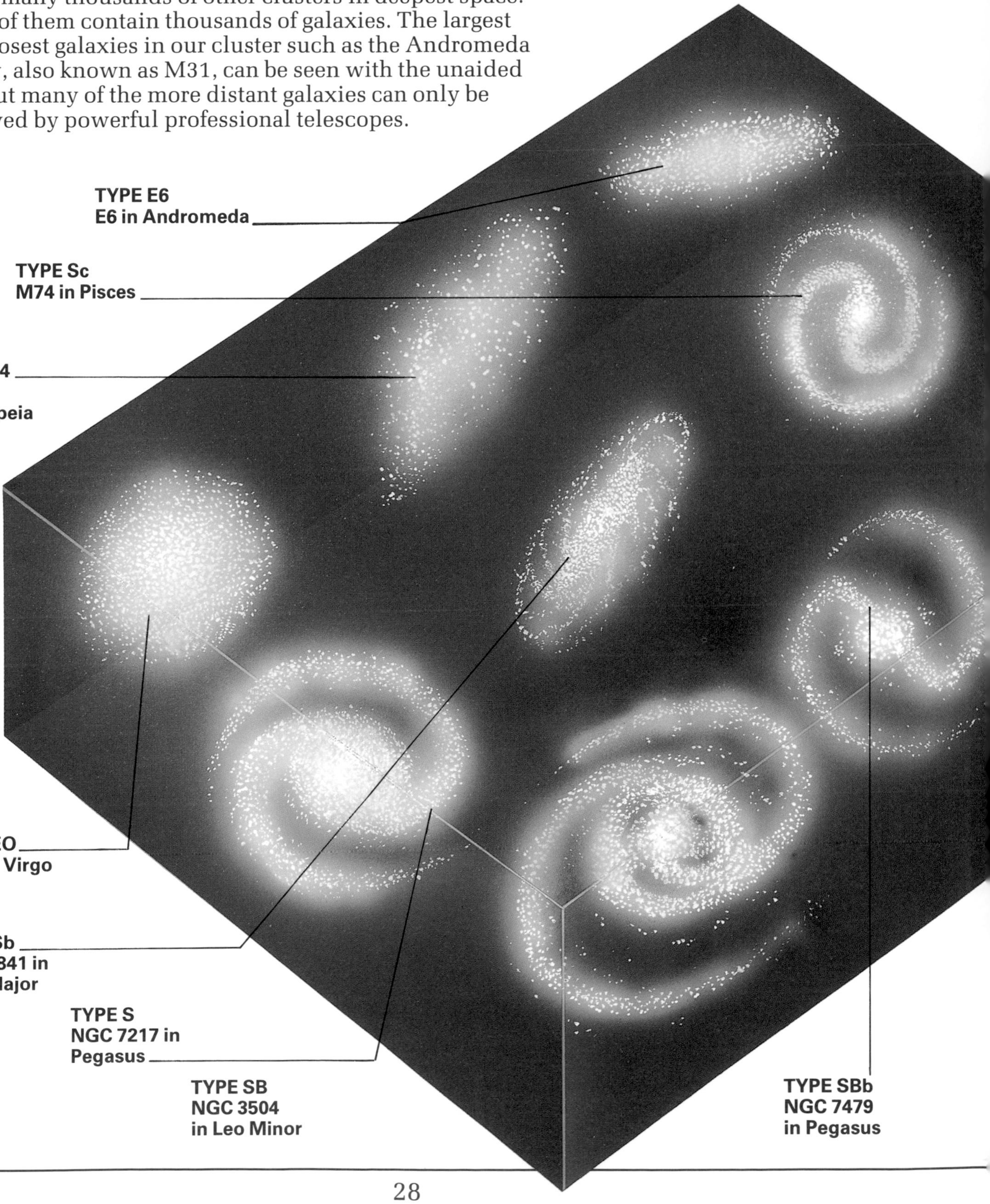

TYPE E6
E6 in Andromeda

TYPE Sc
M74 in Pisces

TYPE E4
E4 in Cassiopeia

TYPE EO
M87 in Virgo

TYPE Sb
NGC 2841 in Ursa Major

TYPE S
NGC 7217 in Pegasus

TYPE SB
NGC 3504 in Leo Minor

TYPE SBb
NGC 7479 in Pegasus

HOW TO SEE

Faint galaxies are easily swamped by light from elsewhere, so choose a very dark, moonless night for observations, and move as far away from house and street lighting as possible. Use a good star map to identify a star close to where the galaxy is located and then examine the area carefully with binoculars or a telescope.

TYPE SBc
NGC 1073
in Cetus

FURTHER TYPES
Although Edwin Hubble first classified the galaxies according to three basic types (see above), astronomers have now found so many variations of these that new codes have had to be developed to describe them all.

THE LATEST DISCOVERY

In June 1991, a British-led team of astronomers revealed they had discovered the most powerful object in the Universe. It is a distant galaxy producing 300 trillion times as much energy as the sun. The astronomers believe that it is either a quasar (see page 25) or a young galaxy which is producing a massive burst of new stars. Their discovery took place after 40 nights of detailed observation into deep space. It is the first such find after a 30-year search conducted by many teams.

OBSERVING GALAXIES

The colorful images of galaxies that appear here were made with the aid of powerful telescopes. A small telescope or binoculars will not reveal as much detail, but they are easy to find. The two closest galaxies to Earth, the Large and Small Magellanic Clouds can be seen from the Southern Hemisphere only. M31 in Andromeda is easily visible from the Northern Hemisphere. Nearby, the fainter M33 can be found in Triangulum.

KEEPING RECORDS

It is always worthwhile to keep a written record of your observations in a notebook used only for that purpose. Note the same details on every occasion – date, time, sky conditions, the type of instrument used, and a paragraph describing what you saw. Astronomers use Universal time, which is the same as Greenwich mean time (GMT), to avoid any confusion resulting from the many different local times around the world. If you make observations from different places, make a note of your location, too. If you take photographs, make sure that you note the camera's aperture and the exposure details.

SKY DIARY
A notebook enables you to build up a record of observations over a long period and, for example, compare the color, brightness, and numbers of stars seen at different times.

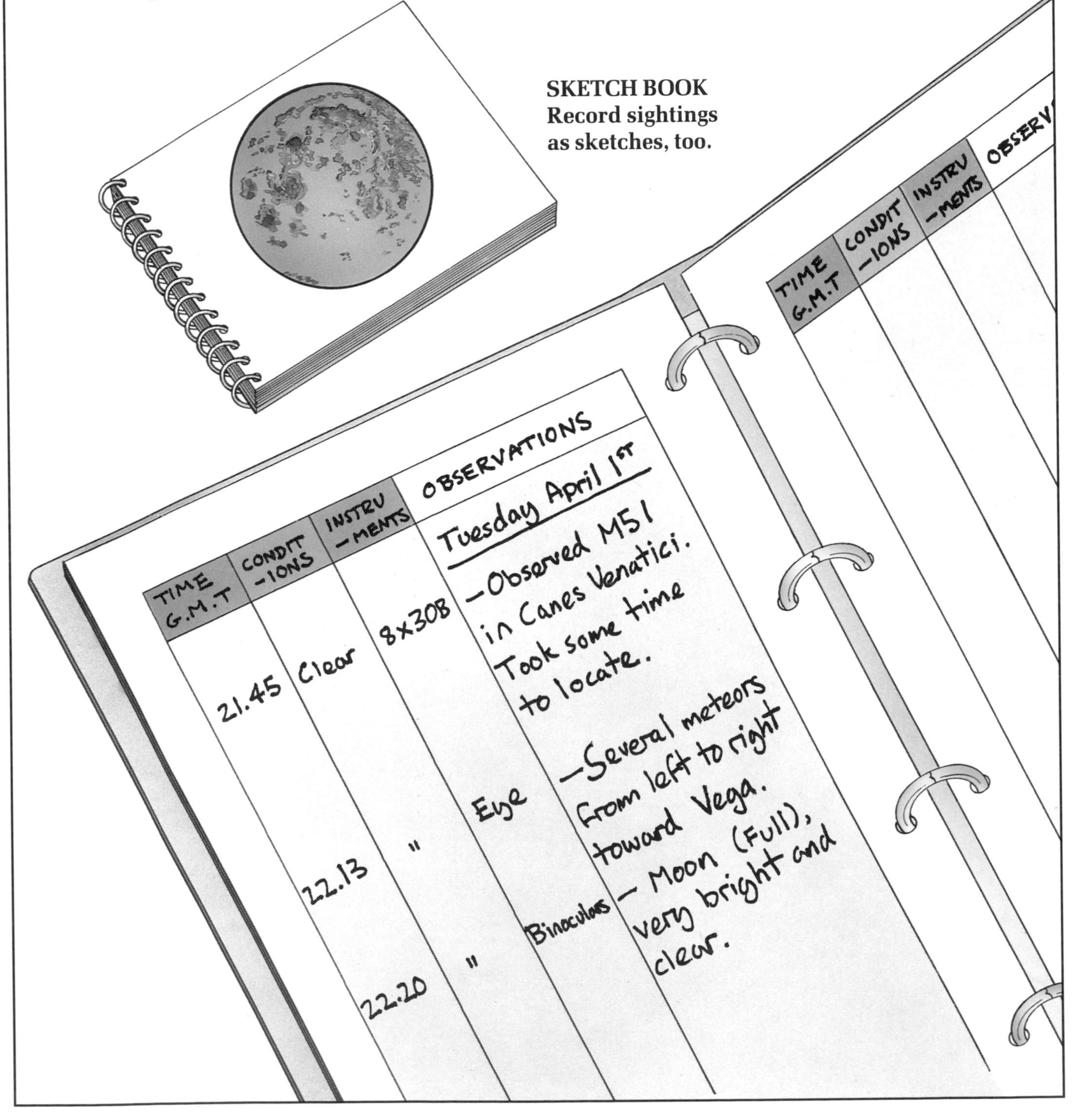

SKETCH BOOK
Record sightings as sketches, too.

KEY DATES IN HISTORY

1608 The refracting telescope is invented by a Dutch lens-maker named Jan Lippershey.
1609 Galileo begins making observations with a refracting telescope.
1668 Sir Isaac Newton builds the first reflecting telescope.
1675 The Royal Greenwich Observatory is founded.
1781 Uranus, the third largest planet, is discovered.
1801 The first asteroid, Ceres, is discovered by Giuseppe Piazzi.
1820 The Astronomical Society of London is formed and later becomes the Royal Astronomical Society.
1840 The first photograph of the moon is taken by J. W. Draper.
1845 The spiral shape of some galaxies is discovered by Lord Rosse at his Birr Castle observatory in Ireland.
1846 Neptune, the fourth largest planet, is discovered.
1850 Stars (Vega and Castor) are photographed for the first time.
1851 Leon Foucault demonstrates the effect of Earth's rotation on a pendulum that hung from the ceiling of the tallest building in Paris.
1923 Edwin Hubble proves that other galaxies exist outside the Milky Way.
1930 Pluto discovered as a result of a search for an object that was disturbing the orbits of Neptune and Uranus.
1931 Experiments by Karl Jansky lead to radio waves from space being detected.
1937 The first radio telescope is built by Grote Reber.
1955 The Jodrell Bank radio telescope is completed.
1957 The beginning of the Space Age – the Soviet Union launches the first artificial satellite, Sputnik 1.
1962 Mariner 2 becomes the first successful space probe to the planets when it flies past Venus.
1967 Pulsars discovered.
1990 The Hubble Space Telescope is launched.

COMMON NAMES OF THE CONSTELLATIONS

Aquarius – The Water Carrier
Aquila – The Eagle
Ara – The Altar
Boötes – The Herdsman
Cancer – The Crab
Canis Major – The Great Dog
Canis Minor – The Little Dog
Capricornus – The Goat
Centaurus – The Centaur
Corvus – The Crow
Crater – The Cup
Crux – The Southern Cross
Cygnus – The Swan
Delphinus – The Dolphin
Dorado – The Swordfish
Draco – The Dragon
Fornax – The Furnace
Gemini – The Twins
Grus – The Crane
Hydra – The Water Monster
Hydrus – The Sea Serpent
Leo – The Lion
Lepus – The Hare
Libra – The Scales
Ophiuchus – The Serpent Bearer
Orion – The Hunter
Pegasus – The Winged Horse
Sagittarius – The Archer
Scorpius – The Scorpion
Taurus – The Bull
Ursa Major – The Great Bear
Ursa Minor – The Little Bear
Virgo – The Virgin

USEFUL ADDRESSES

American Association of Variable Star Observers
25 Birch St.,
Cambridge, MA 02138.

Association of Lunar and Planetary Observers
Box 26,
University Park,
NM 88070.

Astronomial League
3939 Parkcrest Dr.,
NE, Atlanta, GA 30319.

National Deep Sky Observers Society
3123 Radiance Road,
Louisville, KY 40220.

Astronomical Society of New South Wales, PO Box 208, Eastwood, New South Wales 2122.

Astronomical Society of South Australia, PO Box 199, Adelaide, South Australia 5001.

Royal Astronomical Society of New Zealand, PO Box 3181, Wellington C1.

GLOSSARY

Billion In this book a billion is equal to one thousand million.
Black hole A collapsed star whose gravity is so strong that not even light can escape its pull.
Constellation A pattern of stars in the sky that forms a recognizable group from our point of view here on Earth.
Globular cluster A globe-shaped group of old, red stars that are outside the Milky Way.
Gravity The force of attraction between two objects. The more massive an object is the greater its force of gravity.
Light year The distance traveled by light in one year, equivalent to about 5,878,000,000,000 miles.
Magnitude The brightness of a star compared to a standard scale.
Pulsar The dense remains of a collapsed star, emitting radio waves and sometimes other radiation.
Quasar A quasistellar object. A very small and very distant object that is also extremely bright, possibly the brilliant core of a galaxy.
Red giant An old star whose core has collapsed and heated, forcing its outer layers to expand enormously – as much as 300 times the size of the sun.
Reflector A type of telescope invented by Sir Isaac Newton that forms an image by means of mirrors and lenses.
Refractor A type of telescope that forms an image by means of many lenses.
Supernova The massive explosion of a dying star which shines billions of times brighter than an ordinary star
White dwarf The stage after a star has been a red giant. White dwarfs have run out of fuel and are dying.

INDEX